Get

MONEY
SMART

SIMPLE LESSONS TO KICKSTART YOUR
FINANCIAL CONFIDENCE & GROW YOUR WEALTH

ALSO BY
ROBERT PAGLIARINI

The Six Day Financial Makeover
Transform Your Financial Life in Less Than a Week

The Other 8 Hours
Maximize Your Free Time to Create New Wealth and Purpose

The Sudden Wealth Solution
12 Principles to Transform Sudden Wealth Into Lasting Wealth

Get

MONEY
SMART

SIMPLE LESSONS TO KICKSTART YOUR
FINANCIAL CONFIDENCE & GROW YOUR WEALTH

Harbinger Press

ISBN: 978-0-9905715-3-7

This book is printed on acid-free paper.

Printed in the United States of America

Note To The Reader

This book is intended to provide general guidelines that are for informational purposes only and is sold with the understanding that the publisher and author are not engaged in rendering professional services or in providing specific investment advice. The application of general guidelines involving regulatory, accounting, and legal practices, which may differ from locality to locality and which are constantly changing, is highly dependent on an evaluation of individual facts and specific circumstances. With regard to any decisions that can potentially have significant financial, legal, tax, or other consequences, no book can take the place of individualized professional advice. Readers should not regard this book as a substitute for consulting with a competent lawyer, accountant, or other financial professional, as appropriate to the nature of their particular situation. Different types of investments involve varying degrees of risk and there can be no assurance that the future performance of any specific investment, investment strategy, or product discussed in this book will be profitable or suitable for any one reader's portfolio. If readers have any questions regarding the applicability of any investment strategy or product discussed in this book to their particular financial situation, they should consult with a professional advisor.

TABLE OF CONTENTS

Get Money Smart

WHY MONEY SMART

GROW SMART

INVEST SMART

INVEST SMART *Continued*

INVEST SMART *Continued*

INVEST SMART *Continued*

SPEND SMART

SPEND SMART *Continued*

TAX SMART

HELP SMART

HELP SMART

PROTECT SMART

MONEY SMART VIDEO SERIES

BRING THE LESSONS TO LIFE!

WHY GET MONEY SMART

Section 1

PERSONAL MESSAGE
FROM THE AUTHOR

Get Money Smart

As a kid, if you'd have told me I'd have a successful financial planning firm, be the author of several personal finance books, and be a financial professional on TV, I would have said you were crazy. Never in a million years did I think I would be advising people about money. Why?

Growing up, we never had any money! I was raised by a single mom and three older sisters in a small town in the Pacific Northwest. We lived on government cheese and free powdered milk. Every day was a struggle for my mom. She used to sell pieces of our furniture when things got tight. We never used our heater because it was too expensive, so I used to sleep in a sleeping bag in my bed – and still froze! I share this because for the longest time, my background discouraged me. There was no opportunity where I lived and no role models, but looking around, I knew I wanted something different.

I became a student. I spent hours upon hours at the library and Powell's Books in Portland, reading, learning, and growing. I understand the power of a good book and the knowledge that comes with it. If anyone had financial fear, it was me. I didn't know anything about money, but I persevered. I suffered through countless books and courses, taking in nuggets here and there. I overcame my background and my financial fear. This is why this book is so important and personal for me. I understand what it's like to not know the first thing about personal finance. Over the last twenty years, I've dedicated my life to helping people increase their wealth and boost their financial confidence through empowerment and education.

When I was young, I would have laughed at the thought that I would help people "get money smart," but now I understand the gift I was given. There is really nothing like being able to understand the fears and hopes of another person, to be able to empathize and relate to them without judgment.

I was born to write *Get Money Smart*. Financial stress? I saw the stress and anxiety that money issues brought to my mom. She put on a great game face, but the daily money struggles affected her. Do we buy the milk or the bread? What bill should we pay this month? I get it. I know what it's like to think that nothing will ever improve and that wealth and success is for everyone else. It's a horrible feeling that, somehow, the game is rigged and you cannot win. But here is what I know. I'm not special. I'm just a normal guy who happens to know about money. More importantly, I know how to help others who feel worried and hopeless to create a better, fuller, and richer life by learning about and taking control of their finances.

I sincerely hope this book helps you gain financial confidence and success.

INTRODUCTION

Get Money Smart

You Are Either Playing the Game or Getting Played

Make no mistake. If you are not money smart, you are getting ripped off. You are paying too much tax or too much interest (or too much of both!). When you don't know the rules or your options, you can easily get taken advantage of and miss out on all kinds of incredible financial opportunities. Basically, if you're not money smart, you're leaving money on the table.

Are you passing up free money?

If you're like me, I'm guessing you work hard for your money. You get up early, commute, and put in long hours. You make sacrifices and sometimes dedicate your evenings, weekends, and even vacations to your career. You probably spend more time at work than at home with your family or friends. When you are "money smart," your money will work just as hard as you do.

Sometimes all it takes is just minor financial tweaks – doing a few small things a little differently to have a dramatic effect on your overall wealth. I've created hundreds of financial plans for clients in my career. In each financial plan, I analyze where the client is financially, and I share with them new financial strategies they could be doing. The strategies might be things that help them invest better, save more, or reduce the taxes they pay. The difference between no planning and just a little bit of planning is always astonishing. Simply by making a few changes, they often end up with a great deal more wealth and income. It's not just numbers on a page or fancy graphs or charts; there are real people with hopes and dreams behind these numbers.

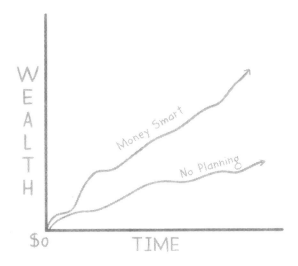

The power of planning

By playing the financial game a little smarter, it means you can live a better life, send your kids to college, take your family on a cruise, pay for your daughter's wedding, and live without fear of running out of money. This is the power of getting money smart. It can better your life and the lives of those you love today, tomorrow, and for generations.

There is a great deal of research that shows the more you know, the faster your wealth grows. Researchers call it "financial literacy," but it basically means that if you have even a basic understanding of money, investing, debt, credit, and taxes, you can make better financial decisions and that these can lead to greater wealth, saving more money, having a higher credit score, paying less interest and lower fees, avoiding common financial pitfalls, being better prepared for retirement, being in better health, and feeling fewer financial concerns[1] (although knowledge doesn't always translate into better behaviors).

The good news is that you don't need to have a Ph.D. in finance to be money smart. It doesn't have to be painful or take years. It just takes a little knowledge for you to play the game and win...

Learn About Money in Minutes, Not Months

Get Money Smart provides a system for rapidly increasing financial knowledge and financial confidence. The system is a one-of-a-kind book and online financial video boot camp that makes a real impact on those who go through it. How do I know? This is the same material and course I have used for years in my nationally-recognized wealth management firm.

But who am I? I have over two decades of experience working to help clients improve their finances and figuring out what works and what doesn't. I've appeared as a financial professional on shows such as *Good Morning America* several times, *20/20, Dr. Phil, Fox Business,* and many others. I'm a Certified Financial Planner™ practitioner and an Enrolled Agent with the IRS. I have a master's degree in personal finance and am currently earning a Ph.D. in financial and retirement planning where I focus on behavioral finance and financial education. However, none of those qualifications are what make this system so effective.

What makes the *Get Money Smart* system special is it was developed not just by a financial professional, but also a behavioral expert. The book and video course were built from the ground up using the latest insights in psychology, motivation, learning, and behavior change.

In addition to a master's degree in personal finance, I also have a master's degree in psychology and specialized training in Solution Focused Brief Therapy, a rapid approach to changing behaviors. After countless therapy sessions with patients paralyzed by anxiety, fears, and deep phobias, I came to the conclusion that the way we try to teach money skills and personal finance is all wrong.

---

[1] Visit http://moneysmartcourse.com to view the research on financial literacy

Ironically, the personal finance books that attempt to teach us are not the solution, but instead they are part of the problem. These books add to the confusion and contribute to the narrative that money and investing is complex and that there is simply too much to learn. Most people have tried to learn about money and investing before, but the only lesson they took away was that personal finance is boring, complicated, and overwhelming. We are intimidated by what we think we need to know. Readers desperately seek financial insight and understanding but are left feeling helpless and more fearful than when they started.

The book you are holding takes a totally different approach. No one likes being chastised and the typical finger-wagging that most people feel when they read a financial book does more harm than good. People are not idiots. You know you should save more money and that you could probably be making smarter financial decisions. Having some Wall Street guy in a suit criticize you isn't the solution. I'm guessing you don't want to be patronized or judged. *Get Money Smart* meets you where you are and explains money and investing so it makes sense (without the guilt or finger-wagging).

Stripped Down Personal Finance

Imagine you are going to be dropped off in the wild and you will need to survive three weeks alone. The good news is that you'll get two hours of survival training. So how are you going to spend those two hours? When there is more information than time, you have to get creative.

It's not important what you know; it's that what you know is important. If your life depended on it, you'd rip away all of the nice-to-know but nonessential information and focus on the necessary survival skills instead. Become an expert? Well, sure, if you had unlimited time and energy, but you don't. But maybe in those two hours you could learn the most important skills in the most important areas that would help you survive.

Guess what? The same is true when it comes to personal finance. My goal is to rapidly take you through a proven system that will strip away the reams of nonessential information and focus on just the most important areas instead.

I took what I learned from my psychology degree and rapid counseling approach and transformed how I worked with clients in my financial planning firm. What I discovered is that there is very little difference between my therapy patients and my financial planning clients. What they fear may be different, but it's the same level of anxiety, the tightness, the sleepless nights, and the sense that there is nothing they can do to eradicate their fear and improve their lives.

Change doesn't have to take years

I've spent hundreds of hours counseling patients. Sometimes, I would only have two or three hours to create lasting change. I realized quickly that traditional therapeutic methods just weren't effective when time was so limited. A new approach was needed that focused on stripping away the nonessentials and addressing the core fears and hurdles to lasting change.

What helps my therapy patients and my financial planning clients, and in fact, the only thing that helps, is assisting them in creating tiny wins that grow their confidence and crowd out their fear.

Get Money Smart shatters the perception that money and personal finance has to be difficult or overwhelming. It destroys the one thing that holds everyone back, financial fear, and provides the one thing we all crave, financial confidence.

Less is more. It's not about cramming information and creating experts, but rather it's about knowing what to leave out and giving you the essentials. I tell my clients that it's not about what we add, it's what we subtract.

Get Money Smart strips the content down to the essentials. If you are a financial advisor or hedge fund trader, it makes sense to go deep, but for the everyday reader struggling to figure out which credit card they should pay off first or the differences between their 401(k) and a Roth IRA, going deep is detrimental to their financial success because the sheer volume of information is overwhelming and too complex.

The *Get Money Smart* system works because I've used it successfully in the most demanding and time critical area within financial planning – sudden wealth. Working with sudden wealth recipients who get millions from a lottery win, sports contract, lawsuit judgment, stock option IPO, or inheritance is an area that is intense and exciting.

Imagine receiving a windfall of $50 million overnight. The immediate joy and excitement would quickly turn to fear and anxiety. These clients are thrust into a chaotic situation where they are forced to make multi-million dollar decisions almost immediately. Their anxiety is high and their financial knowledge is low and the clock is ticking.

As the national recognized thought leader and authority in sudden wealth, I developed the *Get Money Smart* system to get these clients financially knowledgeable and confident as quickly as possible. They do not have years, months, or even weeks. They have a matter of days to rapidly increase their financial knowledge and firmly develop their financial confidence.

Eureka! The key to financial confidence!

Imagine feeling financially scared and unsure, or "financially impotent" as one client remarked, and then after reading the very first lesson of *Get Money Smart*, feeling like you get it for the first time in your life. That you understand how credit, investing, debt, and money works. And that you won't freeze any time you are faced with a financial decision but that you have a greater sense of financial confidence to start making decisions you were always too fearful to make before.

With each lesson you read, you will understand more about money and investing. You will start to make better decisions that will not only boost your financial confidence, but also increase your wealth!

Let's get started!

GROW SMART

Section 2

TYPES OF INCOME

Do you know the two types?

An example of "active" income

What do you think the two types of income are? Does it really matter? Who cares? I mean, income is income. It's all good. Are you really going to hesitate when someone hands you a check while you try to figure out what type of income you are receiving?

I do think it's important to think about income, but for many people, they only think in terms of one kind of income. By knowing that there is more than one form of income, it can help you think differently and help you earn both types of income.

The first type of income is what most people think. It's called "active" income. This is money you get from work. You work a part-time job while you are going to school, or maybe you put in 40 or 50 hours working for a company and you get a paycheck. This is called active income, but it takes effort on your part. When the alarm goes off in the morning, you have to physically get up and go to work to earn your paycheck. And this makes it interesting. It requires your effort and your time. You have a limited amount of effort and time you can give. I mean, how many full-time jobs can you have a week? If you're at Company A working, you can't also be at Company B working. It's one or the other. We all have just 187 hours in a week. Our time is limited – there is a cap on the number of hours we can work for active income. But this is how most people are familiar with income and how most people earn income. They get up, go to work, and get a paycheck. That's active income.

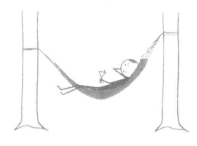

Kick back, relax, and watch your passive income grow

Is there such a thing as non-active income? Yes. It's called passive income. If you're earning passive income and the alarm goes off in the morning, you get to hit the snooze button. Actually, if you earn passive income, you can chuck your alarm out of the window. Buh-bye, alarm clock. Why? Because passive income doesn't require your effort or time. In fact, while your friends are stuck in traffic on the way to their jobs, you get to sleep in and still make money.

Sound too good to be true? Passive income is how many wealthy people make the majority of their income. How? The most common sources of passive income are:

Rental properties. People paying you rent from a house, apartment, or building you rent to them.

Investments. Stocks, bonds, and other investments that pay income.

Royalties. If you write a book or song or invent something, you can get paid a percentage of each sale.

The goal for many is to gradually increase their passive income so they are less dependent on active income. And this often requires working a traditional job and earning active income while you invest and ramp up your passive income.

The takeaway (at this point anyway) is not so much all the different ways to earn active or passive income. The takeaway for you should be that there are actually two types of income: active requires your effort and time, while passive doesn't require very much of your effort or time.

Pop quiz! If a friend said he wants you to start a business with him, is that active or passive? Active for sure. It will require a great deal of your time and effort. If the same friend said he wants to borrow money from you and pay you interest, is that active or passive? Passive. You earn the interest in your sleep and without doing anything. Of course, after your friend stiffs you, it will turn very active as you try to get your money back!

WHAT'S THE BEST WAY TO SAVE?

A story of a banana and a Hershey's Kiss

Most advisors and financial experts will tell you that the only way to become wealthy is to save. The good news is that this is not true. There are ways to become wealthy without saving. For example, you can inherit money, win a lawsuit settlement, start a company with borrowed money and sell it, or start a Ponzi scheme. If the first three are not practical and if you have a conscience and prefer not to spend 10 to 20 years in prison, sadly you will need to save in order to become wealthy.

Why do I say sadly? The problem with saving is that most people get more value and joy from consuming their extra money than they get from saving it. If you fall into this camp, when faced with the choice of getting immediate joy from buying something right now versus saving for some distant time in the future, buying whatever today is a much more attractive choice.

We value now more than we value later.

Here's why saving is so difficult. Imagine you and I were going to meet a week from today. For our meeting, I want to offer you a snack. You can choose a fruit or chocolate. Which one do you want?

When researchers did this experiment, they found that 74% of participants said they wanted fruit a week before the meeting, but on the day of the meeting, 70% decided they wanted chocolate.

So what's going on here? Why did so many people say they wanted fruit only to change their mind to chocolate? It's the same reason why it's so painful to save for the future when instead we could spend the money today.

Those who chose the fruit were trying to make a healthy decision. Since the snack was a week away, it was easier to make a smarter choice. But when it came down to actually eating the snack, most of them changed their minds and decided to go for the less healthy snack instead.

We put a HUGE amount of value on right now and very little value on not right now.

One more quiz…which of these would you prefer:

1. 15 minute massage now

2. 30 minute massage in one day

If you are like most people, you said give me the massage right now (#1).

Okay, how about now?

1. 15 minute massage in seven days

2. 30 minute massage in eight days

Did you choose #2 this time? But why? The massage times are the same and the time between them is the same. What's going on here?

The same effect is at work. We want it now; whatever "it" is – chocolate, massages, spending, etc. Now rules and tomorrow drools. Having a little piece of goodness right now is so much more rewarding than having a whole lot more goodness in the future. Right now has so much more importance than the future that we are willing to experience less as long as we get it right now.

Can you see how this can really screw up our desire and motivation to save? The experts say, "Save your money today so you can have a great retirement," but what we hear is, "Deprive yourself of that awesome thing you can experience right now because in forty years it might help you." Forty years?!?! I don't know what I'm doing in 40 minutes and you want me to hit pause on the joy button because something is going to happen in 40 years?! Not gonna happen.

Does this mean we are destined to spend a lot and save a little? If the choice is between guaranteed enjoyment now versus the possibility of enjoyment a few decades from now, then yes, we're screwed.

So what's the solution? Flip the script by eliminating your choices. This is done by creating a systematic savings strategy. I think willpower is overrated. Rather than to put yourself in a situation where you have to decide between now or later, it's better to avoid the decision altogether.

The solution is generate enough willpower to set up your systematic savings strategy once and then you can forget about it. Here's how you can do it:

Contribute to your 401(k). This is an easy way to save because you set it up once and then it runs automatically without any effort or decisions from you in the future. Basically what happens is that every time you get paid, a small piece of your paycheck gets split off and put into your 401(k). The advantage of this approach is that the money doesn't reach your bank account for you to spend. It also has the benefits of potentially saving you taxes and you may even get free money from your company – called a company match. If you pay little or no income tax, there may be better strategies, but for most people it's a great way to save.

Use direct deposit. Direct deposit is also an easy way to save effortlessly. The advantage is that you only have to make the decision to save once. After it's setup, it will run behind the scenes automatically.

Instead of receiving a check that you have to bring to the bank to deposit (this takes way too much time and willpower), your paycheck can be automatically and directly deposited into a bank or investment account for you.

Take advantage of automatic transfers. If your employer doesn't offer direct deposit, you can still create a systematic savings strategy. Use automatic transfers through your bank to transfer money from your checking to a savings or investment account.

For example, you can tell your bank that you want to schedule an automatic transfer of $200 on the 1st of every month from your checking account to your Schwab investment account. These automatic bank transfers are slightly more time consuming to set up, but once they are, they run automatically without any other effort or action on your part.

Make the most of technology. There are quite a few apps available that can make saving easier. They range from unobtrusive (e.g., rounding up on purchases and saving the difference) to extreme (e.g., pulling money out of your bank account based on the application's algorithm). Because apps and technology change so quickly, the best bet is to search "apps to automatically save money."

How much should you save? I'm so glad you asked...

HOW MUCH TO SAVE?

Here's an easy rule of thumb you'll never forget

Since I'm 20 and just starting out, I only save 10% of my income

I'm older and making more money, so I save 22% of my income

How much should I save? What do you think I should be putting away? What's a good rule of thumb for how much money I should set aside each month? Is there a right amount I should be saving?

This is probably one of the most common personal finance questions, and this causes a great deal of anxiety for people. Most advisors say you should save 10% a year, but there are all kinds of problems with this. It's not customized for the person, and it leaves a lot of cash on the table.

There is always this fear of not saving enough or not knowing if they are on track or not.

Problem solved. I created a very simple but powerful formula that works well for just about anyone.

Save half your age.

That's it. Done.

Here's how it works:

Take your age, divide it by two, and that is how much of your income you should be saving. For example, if you're 20 years old and just starting your first job, you should save 10% of your salary. If you're 44 years old, you should save 22%.

What are the benefits? When you're younger and aren't making much, reaching the target savings rate is easier. When you're older, you're not only saving a greater percentage, but you are presumably making more money and are saving a greater dollar amount.

UNDERSTANDING COMPOUND INTEREST

The secret to exponential growth

Pop Quiz! Compound interest, compound fracture, compound fraction – one of these can help you become filthy rich, and another can guarantee you'll be a slave to debt and broke. Can you guess which is which? Surprise! The answer to both is compound interest. It doesn't seem to make sense, does it? How can compound interest be your FastPass to riches and also your ticket to homelessness?

I love a good riddle, so let's unpack this.

Compound + interest. What does this mean? Well, think of interest as what you get paid as an investor for owning an investment. For example, as an investor, you might get paid the following on these investments:

Bond – if you buy a bond, you get paid income every few months called interest

Real estate – rental income

Stock – dividends

Again, you are getting income because you own the investment. But what could you do with this income you get? Well, you could just leave it as cash. You know, just keep it in your account as good old cashola.

What else could you do with it? You could spend it. That's always an option. I mean, it's your money, so you can buy whatever you want. And this is where things get interesting.

What could you buy with the money you're getting paid as an investor?

New shoes. Upgrade your computer. Remodel the bathroom. Trip to Paris. Yes, yes, yes, and yes. But are we forgetting anything? Couldn't you also buy more of the investment paying you the income?

This is where you get "compounding" from. You are taking the cash you are getting from your investment and buying more of the investment. This means next time you get paid, you get money from the original amount you put in, plus a little extra because your investment is larger.

Let me say this another way. Do you remember the story of Johnny Appleseed? I really hope not because I'm going to make up a lot of stuff about him, so work with me here, would you? Johnny Appleseed was a poor boy. He had no money, but he had a dream. He wanted to be the apple magnate of his time. He got his start washing cars. He barely made enough money to survive, but he was able to save a nickel after many months.

He cut open the apple, took the seeds, and planted them. Twenty years later, his little seeds turned into four apple trees. After the first harvest, he cut open the apples, removed the seeds, and planted those. He did this year after year, planting the seeds from his harvest to increase his farm. His farm grew from that first seed to thousands of apple trees because after each year's harvest, he took some of the seeds and reinvested them to expand his apple empire. Each planted seed grew into a tree, which produced thousands of apples and even more seeds he could plant.

This is compound interest. It's taking your income and using it to build and buy and expand your investment, so the next harvest produces even more. This is the power of compound interest.

So do you see how your investment can grow? It gets to the point where this farm you've cultivated takes on a life of its own and grows and grows.

Okay, so that's the good compound interest, but it has an evil side few people realize. It works the same, but instead of growing your investment, it grows your debt.

The evil side of compound interest? It can work against you and grow your debt

Imagine you owe $10,000 in credit card debt. The nice credit card company understands that life can be tough sometimes, so instead of making you pay off the balance in one month, they let you pay just a fraction of the balance. Isn't that swell? Oh, but you know, they're not a charity, so they will charge you a bit of interest on the balance you haven't paid off. And that interest they charge you, that goes right on the card. And the next month, they charge you interest on not just on the original $10,000 you racked up, but the $10,000 plus the extra interest they charged you. It's compound interest, but this time, instead of increasing your investment, it's increasing your debt! It grows and grows until you're so far in debt that just the interest they are charging you is more than your paycheck. Think about that for a second. Because of compounding interest on debt you owe, every day you get up and go to work, you are actually getting poorer. That's horrible.

The takeaway? Compounding is powerful. It's what creates exponential growth. Compound interest can work for you, creating wealth while you sleep or are on vacation, or it can work against you, digging you further and further into debt. The only difference between these two drastic outcomes? Are you the one lending or the one borrowing? So instead of buying debts, where you are the one paying interest each month, buy assets such as stocks, bonds, and real estate where you earn interest each month.

ASSETS VS. LIABILITIES

Here's how to tell the difference

ASSETS

$ $ $

Assets put money in your pocket

You may find that this is the most valuable lesson in the entire book. It's simple. Deceptively simple, actually. But don't let that deceive you.

Who knows? You may just look at the world differently at the end of this.

Let's get into it. An asset versus a liability. What's the difference, and why does it matter?

An asset is anything that puts money in your pocket. An asset could be a mutual fund that pays you dividends, a rental property that provides monthly income, or your house that appreciates in value . All of these factors put money in your pocket, and this is what makes these assets. Think of an asset as your employee. They are working on your behalf, day and night. Their job description is simple – make you money. That's it.

Assets have value because they make money. Some assets are physical, like an apartment building or a stock (even though a stock is not physical, it represents ownership in a real company, which is physical).

Assets can also be intangible, such as human capital. What's human capital? It's the education, skills, experience, degrees, designations, and talent you have. For example, if you had a Ph.D., a law degree, or a CPA designation, could those things make you money? You bet! Education and skills are assets. They can help you make more money.

Liabilities take money out of your pocket

Okay, so an asset is something, anything really, that puts money in your pocket.

If you had to guess, what do you think a liability is? Yup. Anything that takes money out of your pocket. A liability could be a credit card, car lease, vacation rental, or tardiness on a payment. All of these suck money from you month after month.

Assets pay you. You pay liabilities. Simple stuff, but powerful.

What would happen if you just purchased liabilities? You might have a lot of stuff, but none of the stuff would make you any money, and it would all cost you money to keep.

What would happen if you just bought assets? You'd grow an army of investments that would be dedicated to making you money and growing your net worth.

What's the lesson here? Buy assets and avoid liabilities, of course! That would be ideal! But beyond that, start looking at everything as an asset or a liability. Before you buy anything, make a mental note. Is this going to put money in my pocket, or will this take money from my pocket? Get into the habit of having this quick conversation with yourself each time you're about to buy something. Who knows, maybe it won't change how you buy, but then again, it just might.

6

WHAT'S CASH FLOW?

The powerful key to wealth creation

Cash flow. You might be thinking, "Cash flow? My cash doesn't flow. It trickles." Whatever your cash does, it's a good idea to check your cash flow from time to time because it has a big impact on how quickly your net worth goes up.

Cash flow is simple. You look at the money coming in and you look at the money going out. That's why it's called cash flow. You're tracking the movement of the money. Some comes in from your paycheck, maybe interest from a bond, or a rental property you have. And some goes out, maybe to pay your mortgage, food, or cell phone plan.

Cash flow is simple, but powerful.

The big question is, "Are you making more than you spend each month, or are you spending more than you are making each month?" It's kind of an important question and kind of an important thing to know and keep track of. Why?

Let's say you are spending more than you make a month. First of all, how can you spend more than you make? If you make $5,000 a month, how can you spend $6,000? Sadly, you can (and most people do) by using what? Credit cards! Yup. A credit card lets you buy a lot of stuff today but not have to pay for it for a while. In this way, credit cards, loans, or any debt allow you to spend more money than you have or can make.

By keeping track of your cash flow, you can see if you start to spend more than you make. If you consistently spend more than you make, you will bury yourself in debt, and this will wreak havoc on your financial success in life.

So that's the first reason to focus on and pay attention to your cash flow, to make sure you are not spending more than you make.

But what happens if you are spending less than you make? That's what I like to call financial success. But you'll never guess the three things you can do with that extra money. That's coming up right after you learn about net worth.

7

WHAT'S NET WORTH?

This is your financial score. Are you winning or losing?

Are you ready for an exciting chapter? Don't you just love these guys who make these books trying to sell something? They're all hyped up on who knows what and make it seem like whatever junk they are promoting is the greatest thing on the face of the Earth. "I'm so excited! Thank you for coming here! I have this absolutely amazing, game changing, epic, mind blowing product that will radically change your life. I'm so excited about this product! My blood pressure is going through the roof and I'm going into cardiac arrest, but before I do, let me tell you about, uh, let me see what kind of crap I'm selling today..."

Okay, so this is not one of those Red Bull, Ritalin-infused commercials trying to sell you the latest and greatest new thing. What I have to show you is much more exciting because it truly is a game changer and could radically improve your life. And you have to believe me because you've already bought the book. I'm not selling you anything here. It's all legit. I promise.

Attention is important, but what's more important is focusing our attention on the right things. Here is the first thing you should focus on:

Net Worth. Your net worth is simple. It adds up all the stuff you own and subtracts all the stuff you owe.

This quickly tells you how much you are worth at that moment. It's a snapshot in time that shows how much cash you'd have if you sold everything you own and paid off all your debts. Your net worth is an important number. You want your net worth to increase over time so your assets go up and your liabilities go down. The higher your net worth, the greater your financial security. Your net worth is your financial score. It tells you how you've done and where you currently stand.

Add up all the stuff you own, then subtract all the stuff you owe

You can calculate your net worth yourself fairly easily. You just need to make a list of all your assets and liabilities and then update the figures to track it over time. Of course, there are software programs, websites, and mobile apps that can do this for you as well. It doesn't really matter how you calculate your net worth; it just matters that you are calculating it on a regular basis. I suggest at least twice a year.

8

THE ONLY 3 THINGS YOU CAN DO WITH EXCESS CASH

Most people know one. Some know two.
No one knows all three. Will you?

What do we know about cash flow? It's good. Okay. My work is complete.

Not quite. What else do we know? It's important to look at it once in a while so you can see if you are – no, tell me it's not so – spending more than you are making. You're not? Phew! Okay, we dodged a bullet on that one. So if you are not spending more than you are making, you must be spending less than you are making. I'm liking the sound of this already.

You earn $5,000 a month but only spend $4,000. That's called a surplus or excess reserves. Or where I come from, that's just called *good*. And here's the beauty that most people haven't quite really thought about: what can you do with this extra money? There are just three things.

That's right! Bellagio, Venetian, or the Wynn! Vegas, baby. Vegas! Okay, no. That's not good financial advice, but you could **spend it**. That's the first thing you can do with extra money.

What's the second? Well, if I were a good financial advisor, I might suggest you **save it**. You could put the money in your bank account. You could invest the money in a Vanguard mutual fund. You could buy a tax-free municipal bond.

Okay, so with extra money, you could spend it or save it. But there's one more option you have. Can you guess? You can **pay off debt**. Absolutely. Instead of spending it or saving it, you pay down credit card debt, your mortgage, student loans, car loan, whatever.

Extra cash is powerful. And the other cool thing is how your cash flow is connected to, and affects, your net worth. They are bound together. What happens to one affects the other. Or as Dr. Phil would say, they are in a co-dependent relationship. How's that working for ya?

Spend it (no change).

Save it (cash comes in, or goes to investments, net worth up).

Pay it down (cash reduces liability, net worth up).

The only 3 things you can do with excess cash

To track your cash flow, it's easiest to use an online program, such as Mint.com, or software, such as Quicken. These programs make it easy to see what you're bringing in and what's going out. Aim to review your cash flow each month.

Turn your finances into a game. Your goal should be to increase your net worth. By reviewing your cash flow, you can make better decisions. If you notice you are spending what you're making, or worse, spending more than you are making, you can see your net worth start to go down. But, hopefully, this awareness will then cause you to make different decisions. Spend a little less so you have that extra cash at the end of each month. That extra cash is powerful. It can be used to buy more investments or pay down debt. Either way, your net worth goes up.

Want to know something else that is cool? Have you heard of the mysterious blue line? Of course you haven't. That's why it's mysterious! But you will next...

THE THIN BLUE LINE

A large group of NFL players loved this concept

Are you ready for some high level stuff? I think you're ready for it. I don't share what I'm about ready to share with just anyone. I reserve it for special people and special occasions. I think you're the person and this is the occasion.

The first time I shared this was in a small dark room in Las Vegas with about 60 NFL players.

Your ticket to financial freedom

The blue line. What is it, and why could it be one of the most important things you should track? Let's find out.

The thin blue line is the amount of money your money makes. The blue line visually shows you how much you can safely withdraw from your investments each year without running out of money. This is an important concept, so let's make sure you really understand it.

In a later lesson, I will talk about the 4% rule. Basically, we want to know how much we can withdraw from our investments without the fear that we are spending down our investment accounts.

Although some investors are obsessed over calculating their net worth, I think there is no more important number than what the blue line represents.

By calculating and tracking what you could withdraw from your portfolio and live on, along with your income from other sources, such as rental income or Social Security, you will know when the income from your investments could replace the income from your job.

This blue line is your freedom! This blue line shows your level of financial independence. The higher the blue line, the more money you are making from non-work activities, what we call passive activities.

The blue line is super important, and I've found that people really can get into it. On some level, you can understand what your net worth is, but it's hard to really get your head around what it means. Okay, I own this and owe that. But what does that mean in the real world? The blue line is the real world. It tells you exactly how much money your assets make for you. That's something that makes sense and something you can get excited about tracking and increasing because when you increase your blue line it increases your chance at financial independence...

WHAT IS FINANCIAL INDEPENDENCE?

This is what it's all about…

What is financial independence? Well, what's financial dependence? Independence versus dependence. Good versus evil! Independence is always better than dependence, right? The 4th of July is Independence Day! That's good. If your boyfriend or girlfriend ever says, "I like you, but you're really dependent," you can be sure you'll soon be hearing the "It's not you, it's me" breakup speech.

Financial dependence means you are depending on something, but what? You are depending on the income you make from working to pay your bills and to live. To rent an apartment, pay your car loan, and buy food, you need to depend on the money you earn from your job. That's financial dependence, and it's how most people live.

Contrast that with financial independence. Financial independence is about having enough investments so you don't have to work another day in your life. It is where you are not depending on your salary from work to pay your bills. Although you may still decide you want to work, you are not required to work to support your lifestyle. You have the choice to work or not.

What do you need to be financially independent? Financial independence involves earning enough passive income to support the kind of lifestyle you desire. Financial independence is not about being "rich." To be rich, you only need to make or have a lot of money. As a result, there is no "magic" amount of passive income required — it is entirely dependent on your expenses. Let me show you a couple of examples of how this works.

If you earn $100,000 in annual passive income and have expenses of $85,000 per year, you are financially independent. If you have $500,000 in annual passive income but have $750,000 in expenses per year, you are not financially independent.

Therefore, financial independence is having enough income coming from passive sources, such as rental income and your investment portfolio, to pay for your desired lifestyle.

Blah, blah, blah. Okay. You get it? How about we talk about something more exciting than saving? Something really just cool and hip. Like an emergency fund!

Really? Seriously? Are we out of good material? Not yet. Because this is one emergency fund that is unlike any you've heard of.

WHAT'S AN EMERGENCY FUND?

Don't listen to the experts...

First things first. What's a rainy day emergency fund? It's simply some money you've set aside just in case of an unexpected situation where money can help, such as a job layoff, needed medical treatment, or bail (it happens!).

And really, can't most negative and unforeseen events benefit from a bit of money? It's rare you would hear, "I'm sorry, I have a real problem on my hands here and I'd really appreciate it if you'd stop trying to give me money."

No, most of the time, money is exactly what is needed to at least temporarily solve the problem or better the situation. Sometimes, we need to get out of a jam, and money can help. If you lose your job, it's nice to have a cushion to pay the rent and buy food. It's important to have the ability to pay high medical deductibles if you get hurt or sick. If you get a flat tire on the way to work, you need to be able to get it fixed and get back on the road. Stuff happens, and money can certainly help in an emergency by providing options and getting the help you need.

So you definitely need an emergency fund, and most experts say you should have six to 12 months of living expenses in cash. What does this mean? Basically, you would make a list of your essential living expenses, such as rent, insurance, etc. Total just the essentials, and the goal is to have several months of cash available to cover these.

But actually, that's not the goal. In fact, and this is where I'll probably get into trouble. Most financial experts are wrong. I'll give you a million reasons why...in the next lesson.

12

HOW NOT TO SAVE FOR AN EMERGENCY FUND

Do this and you may lose $1 million

The sequel. In the first part, I left off with what we call a cliffhanger in the movie business. Do you remember? I told you most experts get it wrong when it comes to an emergency fund. In fact, I said I'd give you a million reasons why these experts are wrong.

The financial planner police (yes, they exist!) might kick me out of the industry if I suggested it was not important to have the ability to cover these emergency situations. But the antiquated six to 12 months in a checking account or money market account is a terrible idea.

Consider a 30-year-old couple. They're doing their best to save for retirement and raise a family. They calculate that 12 months of living expenses is $75,000. Like good students, they follow the standard financial advice and set aside $75,000 in a savings account at a bank. After a few high fives, they go on about their lives feeling good about their "smart" financial decision. It's too bad, though – they just cost themselves $1 million.

Here's the math:[1]

Traditional Emergency Reserve	Alternative Emergency Reserve
$75,000 in savings account	$75,000 in diversified investment portfolio
1% interest rate	8% investment return
35 years (until age 65)	35 years (until age 65)
TOTAL: $106,245	TOTAL: $1,108,900
Difference: $1,002,655	

---

[1] This is a hypothetical example that is demonstrating a mathematical principle. It does not illustrate any investment products and does not show past or future performance. Investing involves risk, including the loss of principal.

The difference between the emergency reserve savings account and the alternative account is a whopping $1 million!

The "alternative emergency reserve" is simply to invest the cash in a diversified investment portfolio. "But hold on," you say. "Where's the rainy day fund when you need access to money quickly?" You absolutely should have access to assets, cash, or some way to cover these emergencies, but there are many other sources you could access that won't cost you a $1 million at retirement. Here are just a few:

Home equity line. If you own a home, apply for a home equity line of credit. If approved, you will get a checkbook from which you can write checks if you have an emergency.

401(k) loan. Check with your employer to see if your 401(k) allows for loans. You can withdraw 50% of your balance up to a maximum of $50,000, or if your 401(k) balance is $10,000 or less, you can borrow the full amount. You should avoid borrowing from your 401(k) and only consider it as a last resort.

Credit cards. This is often the quickest way to access cash or pay for an emergency – often even faster and more convenient than withdrawing cash from a traditional emergency reserve account.

Investment account. As long as you don't have illiquid investments, the $75,000 you invest can be accessed within a day or two at most.

The takeaway isn't that having an emergency reserve is a bad idea – it's imperative that you have access to a source of funds that you can tap into quickly. The takeaway is that if you keep your emergency reserve assets in cash, a savings account, or money market, you get so little interest or return on this money. I call this a dead asset.

Instead, make sure you have access to assets if there is an emergency. Maybe set aside a few thousand in cash, but take the rest you would have set aside and invest it. Over time, and in this case, 35 years, there is a good chance you'll do a lot better than if it just sat in your checking account.

13

BEING YOUR OWN BOSS VS. WORKING FOR THE MAN

The differences between a 1099 independent contractor
and a W-2 employee

If you work for somebody, there's a good chance you are either an employee or an independent contractor. Is there a difference and does it matter? Yes and yes.

Most people with a job are an employee. This means you show up at a particular time, do your work, have a boss, and get paid a certain amount per hour or week.

If you're an employee you typically get paid each week or maybe twice a month. At the end of the year, the company totals what you made and reports this information to you (and the IRS) on a form called a W-2.

The advantages of being an employee are that you have a pretty good idea how much you are going to make a month and have some job stability. You may even have some company perks like free or reduced cost health insurance, a paid cell phone, access to a 401(k), and even paid vacation time. Of course, if you work for a cool tech company you might get free massages and access to onsite gourmet cafes and bowling!

Want to know what company perk I got at my first job? I had the privilege of being able to buy, yes buy, old pies the restaurant couldn't sell. Move over Google with your fancy onsite barber shop, laundromat, and fine cuisine. I got stale pie. Nothing says we value you like charging for spoiled baked goods.

An employee has a tight relationship with her employer. The employer is legally bound to do certain things for their employees. There are federal and state regulations that control the rules of the relationship, such as the minimum amount the employer can pay an employee, work hours, safety, etc. There is a level of commitment to the relationship.

Okay, so if the employee and employer relationship is like "going steady," then the independent contractor relationship is like having a fling.

An independent contractor still has a "job" and still gets paid but the relationship is a little different. The "independent" in independent contractor means that the person is hired by a company but there are less controls and regulations. If you're an employee you may need to get approval from the company to work another job. If you're an independent contractor, you can do whatever you want. Can you say "hall pass?"

An independent contractor can have more flexibility and freedom in the job they perform, where they perform it, and when they perform it. There are no rules on how much you get paid or overtime hours. The company won't give you health insurance or access to their 401(k) plan. Independent means just that. You are a hired hand that comes in and does a job. Instead of getting a W-2 that reports your income, when you are an independent contractor you get a form called a 1099.

If you think it sounds like it would be better to be an employee, I think most people would agree with you. Of course, the Smurfs movie made over half a billion dollars, so popularity isn't always a good guide for what's good!

As an independent contractor you have your own business – it's you! You can market your services to other companies. For example, instead of working in accounting as an employee, you could use your same accounting skills but be an independent contractor for ten different companies. You can set your own hours and charge whatever the companies will pay you.

It's true that as an independent contractor you may not get all of the perks you might as an employee like health insurance or a 401(k), but as a business owner, you can set up your own retirement plan and give yourself your own benefits. There are also a lot more options to use business expenses as deductions to reduce your taxes.

As the so-called "flex economy" grows, more and more people are either choosing or being forced to become independent contractors. Some people are an employee by day and work as an independent contractor by night such as driving for Uber.

The real lesson is to understand the difference between the two so you can better evaluate any opportunities that come your way.

Whether you are an independent contractor or an employee, in the next chapter you'll learn how to get financially organized...

KEEPING TRACK OF ALL YOUR FINANCIAL STUFF

A simple strategy to not get overwhelmed

Here's the thing. I hate paperwork. I hate organizing stuff. Which makes me the perfect person to be teaching this lesson. Why? If you're like me, the last thing you want is some peppy "I just love and live to organize everything" guy. I can't relate to that. I want someone who says, "Listen, I suck at organizing, but here's what I do and it works pretty well." That's me.

This stuff doesn't have to be rocket science. You just need to do it a couple of times and then get into the habit. And that's probably the real lesson right there. It doesn't really matter how you organize your documents, but that you do and you're consistent.

There are quite a few documents and it can become overwhelming pretty quickly. So start with a game plan. Your first decision is do you want to be a paper guy or an electronic file guy? I'd choose one or the other just to make it easy. Whatever you decide, how you organize your files are going to be the same.

Here are the different categories I would create either in a file cabinet or computer folders:

Insurance: health insurance, auto insurance, home insurance, etc.

Investments: applications you've signed, agreements with investment advisors, monthly statements, etc.

Legal: wills and trusts, power of attorney, etc.

Tax: tax returns, 1099s, charitable donations.

Debt: mortgage paperwork, credit card statements, student loans.

Those are the main categories, but under those, you can have sub-folders to make things even easier to find later.

When it comes to taxes, here's what I like to do. Create a file if you're doing real paper documents or folder if you're keeping everything electronically and label it **Taxes Year**. Within that folder, I have sub-folders labeled **Charitable Receipts, Income, and 1099s**. This makes it easy come tax time to pull this out and have everything in one place to give to your tax person or to help you do your own taxes. It's a huge time saver.

Just get into a habit with these documents. If you're going the paper route, get a **Pending** folder and dump all the financially related mail you get into it and then you can go through it and separate each piece into the different categories later. I like this idea of having a temporary bucket, so to speak, where you dump everything and then can go back through it later. If you're going paperless, create a temporary folder and drag documents into it for the month.

And then, at the end of each month, make a date to go through and clear out the temp folder and file the documents where they belong.

Once you get into the swing of things, it will be effortless, I promise!

WHAT'S INFLATION?

The silent wealth killer

When I was a kid, I had to walk to school in three feet of snow, in June, uphill both ways. Okay, so maybe Gramps is exaggerating just a bit, but when he complains about paying $15 for a movie or $10 for a hamburger because when he was growing up "movies were a nickel and hamburgers were a dime," it may not be such an exaggeration.

If a movie really was a nickel 60 years ago (and by the way, they were), it begs the question why? Is it because movies today are so much better? A quick stop at your local Cineplex can help you answer this.

Why were movies, or hamburgers, or cars, or whatever so much less expensive? The short answer is inflation. The long answer is the rest of this lesson.

Let's break this down. Inflation sounds a lot like inflate, like inflating a balloon. And that's exactly what's happening. Inflation is when the cost of goods or services increases over time. That's the what, but you still don't know the why. Why do prices go up? There are lots of reasons, but I will discuss the main two.

Let's say you have a protein-infused wheat grass stand (I mean, who's buying lemonade anymore?). You charge $5 for a shot of the green sludge and you make pretty good money. Then one day there is a breaking news alert that protein-infused wheat grass cures cancer and heart disease. Suddenly there is a line around the block to buy your stuff. What do you do? Do you lower the price because you are generous and want to help your community? Of course not! You jack up the price to $7.50 a shot and you still sell out. What just happened? Lots of people wanted your product and they were happy to pay more for it. In economist speak, there was increased demand for your product, which enabled you to raise prices. This is one way we get inflation – demand grows faster than supply.

You're making a killing with your protein-infused wheat grass stand. This catches the eye of a few more entrepreneurs who want to make a quick buck. They start buying protein and wheat grass by the carton and bushel. Every day you sell out so you place larger orders of the ingredients. Things are going fine until a big storm destroys 50% of the wheat grass farms. When you place your next order, you see that the cost of wheat grass has shot up by 100%. What do you do? You need the wheat grass, so you buy it. Now that you are paying so much more for the ingredients, you are making a lot less on every shot. So what's a good capitalistic entrepreneur to do? Raise prices! This is the second way we get inflation. When a company's costs go up, they tend to increase their prices to offset the extra expense. But if you're a company, it doesn't look good if you keep raising your prices. Understandably, it might upset a lot of your customers if you're always jacking up the cost. This is where companies get tricky. Rather than raise the cost of a box of cereal, what if they just charged the same but gave you less? They wouldn't dare . . . would they? Oh yes they would! It happens all the time across a variety of products. It's not your imagination – there is more air and fewer chips in the bag, fewer sheets of paper towels, and as one reporter wrote, "Even smaller squares of toilet paper."

You may have a couple of questions. Like, how much do things generally go up each year? Looking back over the past 100 years or so, it's gone up, on average, a little over 3% per year. This means that if something costs $100 this year and there is inflation of 3%, that same thing might cost $103 the next year.

Is there a problem with inflation? Yes and no. Economists say it is important and natural to have some level of inflation, but if you do the Money Smart thing and save your money, it loses its value each year. The $100 you save this year can't buy as much next year or two years from now or two decades from now. This is called the erosion of buying power and it's why inflation is a wealth killer. It's like carbon monoxide – silent, odorless, and invisible. Slowly and gradually your savings are worth less and less. That's the bad news. The good news is there's a solution! It's called investing. Here's how it looks.

Year	Bank Account Balance	What $100 Can Purchase	Investment Account Balance
	(earning 0% a year)	(based on 3% inflation)	(earning 10% a year)
1	$100	$100	$100
2	$100	$97	$110
3	$100	$94	$121
4	$100	$91	$133
5	$100	$89	$146
10	$100	$76	$236
20	$100	$56	$612
30	$100	$41	$1,586
40	$100	$30	$4,114

This is a hypothetical example that is demonstrating a mathematical principle. It does not illustrate any investment products and does not show past or future performance of any specific investment.

What's the takeaway? Inflation is a wealth killer, so you're better off spending all of your savings right away! No, that's not the takeaway. Inflation is a wealth killer, but fortunately there is a way for your money to not just "keep up" with inflation but actually grow faster than inflation. This is called investing and that's what the next section is all about!

INVEST SMART

Section 3

IS INVESTING LIKE GAMBLING IN VEGAS?

What every new investor needs to know

I get this question a lot, and I can understand why. From an outsider's perspective, someone not in the financial or investment industry, I can only imagine how ridiculous it must look.

I remember watching the movie *Trading Places* when I was a kid. It's the film where Eddie Murphy plays a homeless hustler and gets the opportunity to be a commodity investment trader overnight. Come to think of it, that was a hard R-rated movie and it came out when I was, like, ten. What's up with that, Mom? So much for parental supervision. When you're the youngest of five kids, *parental* and *supervision* were two words I had no concept of as a child. And for that, I thank you, Mother!

Anyway, back to the film filled with profanity, drugs, nudity, and prostitution. I remember Eddie was trading orange juice futures contracts and it all seemed so absurd. Prices would go up, down, and all over. There was no rhyme or reason, it seemed. It was all luck. It looked like it was one big roll of the dice.

And this may be how you think of investing. If you watch CNBC or Fox Business, or read some of the financial websites, it can all seem so arbitrary. Again, like you are in Vegas playing roulette: spin the ball and hope for the best.

In some ways, that's a pretty good description of the stock market, but only in the short-term. What the market does day-to-day or even week-to-week is anyone's guess and gamble. Red? Black? Market going up? Down? It's all about the same. When I was explaining this to a client once, she said, "What's the point then? At least in Vegas I get free drinks!"

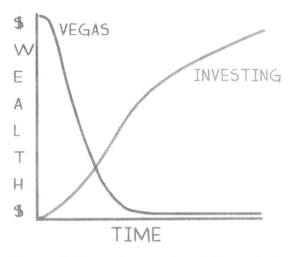

Successful investing requires skill, not luck

But fear not. Although the day-to-day movement of the stock market or a particular stock is just about as predictable as a slot machine, over longer periods, investing has almost nothing to do with luck and everything to do with skill and patience.

Let's go back to our roulette example. When you put your chips on 33, you have no edge. Where the little white ball ultimately lands is purely luck. You get lucky and win big, or you don't and lose everything.

Now compare that to investing. Instead of putting your chips on number 33, you put your money into a stock like Apple. What does that mean, though? It means you are buying a piece of Apple, the company. It means you own a little bit of the company. You have ownership in a company that makes products and sells them all over the world. You have ownership in a company that earns billions of dollars a year and employs 100,000 people who are researching and designing new products they can sell. You have ownership in a business that may continue to make money and grow. As an owner, you benefit from every iPhone they sell. It's no different than if you had your own company you owned by yourself. Every sale you made and all the profit would benefit you. However, since you don't own 100%

of Apple, you share in the success of the company with everyone else who owns Apple stock.

Now compare this to the roulette ball and hoping it lands on your number. Vegas can be a blast. I've never been much of a gambler, but I understand the momentary thrill of anticipation of hitting 21 or busting. But investing is not gambling. Vegas requires luck, whereas investing requires skill and patience.

In Vegas, you are betting on a ball, a die, or a card. As an investor, you are betting on products, people, and future profits. And if you do well, you can afford to buy your own drinks!

But how? How exactly do you, as an investor, make money? There are two glorious ways and most people can't name both of them. Can you?

TWO WAYS TO MAKE MONEY AS AN INVESTOR

Most people get this wrong

Investing is good.

Well, yes, but why is investing good?

Uh, because you make money?

Yes, that's true, and how do you make money as an investor?

As an investor, you invest and this investing makes investment money. It's common knowledge.

I've asked a lot of people over the years how an investment can make money and few can quickly tell me.

As an investor, you can make money in two different ways.

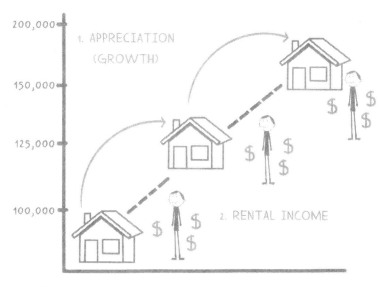

Two different ways you can make money from an investment

Imagine you buy a house that you to rent to a nice family, maybe a young aspiring artist, or maybe Walter White. Whatever, it doesn't matter who you rent the house to. Let's just say you rent it to someone.

What are they going to send you each month? Well, unless they are deadbeats, they will send you a rent check. They will pay you income for being able to rent your house. This is the first way you can make money as an investor, by getting income from your investment.

This income can be called different things depending on what you invest in. For example, if you buy a bond or invest in a CD, this would be called interest. If you invest in a stock that pays income, it would be called a dividend. Doesn't really matter what you call it. It's all just income. You are getting paid rent, so to speak, because you own the investment.

So, the first way to earn money as an investor is from income – rent, dividends, interest – whatever you want to call it.

Back to your rental house. Those monthly rent checks are nice, but now let's also suppose the value of the house goes up. Maybe you bought it for $100,000, and now because Justin Bieber *moved out* (yes, moved out!) of the neighborhood, prices skyrocketed. Now if you were to sell your house, you could get $150,000. This is the second way to make money as an investor. The price of whatever you invested in could go up.

This is also called appreciation, growth, or capital gain, and it's not limited to your rental house. Let's say you bought a stock for $10 and now it is worth $15. That $5 that it went up in value is appreciation.

Sometimes an investment, like your rental house, may provide both income and appreciation, but some investments only provide one or the other. That's okay, too.

These are the two primary ways an investor can make money: **income** and **appreciation**.

If your investment doesn't provide either of these, it's probably not much of an investment.

Before you start investing your money, let's learn a bit about stocks in the next lesson. Plus, you'll learn how I disappointed my daughter at Disneyland. Good times.

UH, WHAT'S A STOCK?

Capitalism 101

As an investor, my guess is a good deal of your portfolio will be in stocks and bonds. These are the two primary types of investments for most investors.

Knowing the differences is critical in your journey to being truly money smart.

You may already have a good grasp of what a stock and bond is, but stick with me for this short lesson, as there might be a nugget or two of new information you'll learn.

Okay, what's a stock? A stock is ownership in a company. Alrighty then, what's a company? A company is a separate legal entity that exists apart from its owners. Although the owners of a company are mortal, a company is eternal. Think about Apple – the company, not the fruit. Steve Jobs passed away, but we still get the new versions of the iPhone because the company continues to live. A company is like a person in that it has certain rights and responsibilities – again, separate and distinct from its owners. And unless you live in certain progressive countries such as the Netherlands, New Zealand, or Germany, another key difference is a company can legally sell itself but a person cannot. This is where the idea of stock comes in.

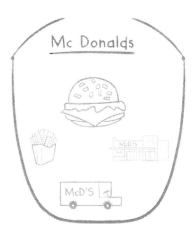

As a shareholder you own a small piece of everything a company owns

It's kind of simple, if you think about it. When a company is started, the owner or owners decide how many shares of stock the company should have. It could be just one share or it could be a million shares. And they can change their mind and start with one share and then change it to more later.

Although a company, such as McDonald's, can own lots of stuff like buildings, trucks, and French fries, the company itself is its stock. If you want to invest in McDonald's, you don't buy a vat of their special sauce; you buy shares of McDonald's stock. And by having just a single share of McDonald's stock, you actually own a small piece of not just their not-so-special sauce, but everything the company owns. That's cool, isn't it?

But why would you want to own stock in a company? You want to make money, of course! How? You expect the company to make lots of money. You expect them to sell lots of burgers and shakes. If they do, then your little slice of ownership becomes more valuable. But keep in mind that when you own something, it can go down in value. Stocks can lose money. There are other kinds of investments that don't lose money, but as a stockholder or shareholder, you definitely could lose money.

Stock, also called equity, is ownership. As a stockholder, as an owner, you get special rights. You get to vote on important company matters, show up for their annual meetings, and even get income in the form of dividends from their profits. But, sorry, you don't get a complimentary Big Mac.

This is a painful reminder of the time I took my daughter to Disneyland. I told her we owned Disney stock, which meant we owned a small piece of Disneyland. The initial look of admiration on my daughter's face was what a parent longs for, but it quickly faded after I told her this didn't mean we could get a free Mickey Mouse pretzel.

You could do many things with your money, but when you invest in a stock or stocks, you are making an educated decision and placing your money on the management of the company, the people who work there, the new products or services they are going to offer, and their profits. In essence, you are investing in the future success and growth of the company.

If that's a stock, then what's a bond? Let's just say it's something completely different.

UH, WHAT'S A BOND?

It's simple if you think about it like this…

In the last lesson, you learned about stocks, which is ownership in a company. What's a bond then? Well, it's not ownership. Instead, it's an IOU.

Imagine you have a friend who needs to borrow $1,000 from you. If you lend her the money, she gets the cash and you get what? A grateful friend, but what else? You get her promise to pay you back. Yeah, she gets cold hard cash and you get a promise? Yup, that's pretty much what a bond is. It's a promise to pay you back.

It's not just friends who are hard up that come looking to borrow money. Companies borrow money, too. When they borrow money, they issue these IOUs called bonds. They are promises to pay back all the people who lend them money. Get it? It's a bond, a sense of togetherness, to be joined. You and the company now are joined and have a bond.

But unlike a friend, where you may lend them a $100 and tell them to give you a $100 back, if you lend a company money, you're going to want more than just your $100 back. I mean, why would you give some company your money just so you can get the same amount of money back? Well, you wouldn't. You'd want to get a little (or maybe a lot) more back.

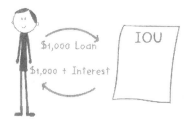

Bonds are IOUs from a company. They pay your initial investment, plus interest

This is why people invest in bonds. Here's how it works. You lend the company money and the company promises not only to pay you back, but along the way, they will give you a little more. This "little more" is what is called interest. So you lend a company $1,000, and you agree that the company has to pay you back the original amount you lent them in one year, which is called the principal. In addition, the company will give you an extra $100. This extra $100 is the interest.

Bonds are also called fixed income. Why? Usually, when you own a bond, you get these interest payments every six months. So, in that example, they would give you $50 after the first six months and then $1,050 at the end of the year. Why $1,050? The $1,000 was your original principal, and the extra $50 was the second interest payment.

Unlike a stock where you have real ownership in the company, when you own a bond, you have no ownership in the company. Just like when a friend borrows money from you, you don't own them. You just have their promise to pay you back. That's what you own, a piece of paper that says, "I owe you such and such."

Can you lose money? You bet. If the company breaks their promise and decides they can't pay you back, then you might not get the money you lent them. That's a real risk.

Capeesh? Or Capiche? Or Capische? Whatever. Do you understand?

Quick recap. A bond is a promise to pay you back what you lend a company, plus a little extra called interest. You don't own any part of the company when you own a bond. You just own the IOU, the piece of paper with their promise.

Okay, you get stocks and bonds now, but which is better for you to invest in? You'll learn the answer to that question next.

WHAT ARE BETTER, STOCKS OR BONDS?

Why you need both to create wealth

It's kind of like asking, "What's better, chocolate or vanilla ice cream?" Both are great for different reasons.

First, why stocks? Well, stocks are ownership. This means if the company sells a lot of stuff, expands into different countries, and makes a lot of money, you get to go along for the ride. Your little piece of ownership goes up with the company.

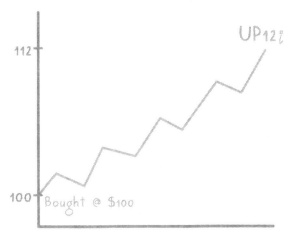

An example of stock appreciation

As an owner in the company, you may get part of the profits. Pop quiz! Do you remember what these were called? They are called dividends. You may get some of the profits through dividends, which are just cash payments. And if the company does well, the price of the stock may increase in value. Just like the price of a house can go up in value, the stock can go up in value, too. This is called growth or appreciation.

If you look back in time over many years, on average, stocks have gone up around 12% per year. This means if you invest $100 in a stock and it goes up 12%, then at the end of the year, you have $112. But these are averages across all stocks. Some went up much more than 12%. For example, Apple stock has gone up 44% each year on average over ten years, starting in 2002. Of course, not all stocks are Apple and not all stocks go up 44% a year, or even 12% a year. In fact, some stocks didn't go up at all. They went down. And some went out of business. Think about companies such as Circuit City, Blockbuster Video, Best Buy, RadioShack, and others. Not all companies continue to produce things the public wants.

Stocks fluctuate a great deal. They can be up 12% one year and down 20% the next. The technical term for this roller-coaster-ride instability is volatility. Lots of ups and downs. But with patience and over longer periods, stocks are one of the best performing investments you can have.

What about bonds? Well, bonds are quite different.

Remember, while a stock is ownership in the future success of the company, a bond is just a promise from the company that they will pay you back the money they borrowed from you and throw in a little extra money called interest.

Why bonds then? Well, they tend to be more stable. They aren't up and down drastically like stocks, meaning they are less volatile. The big benefit of a bond is you get stable income. You know you will get a certain amount of interest every six months. With a stock, who knows? Nothing is guaranteed. With a bond, you have an agreement that commits the company to paying you. This is a big draw for bond investors. They like the stability and they like the cash flow. And even better, if the company goes out of business, the bondholders get their money back before the stock owners. How do you like that? As a stock owner, you have to wait until everyone else is paid back before you get anything. As a bond owner, you get your money back first. Again, that's stability and security. That's what a bond provides.

So, what is better? Both stocks and bonds have vastly different characteristics with different benefits. Stocks are for growth. Bonds are for income. They both have a place in everyone's portfolio.

It's been said that stocks are like girlfriends and bonds are like buddies. Actually, no, that's never been said. I made it up, but in the next lesson, you'll learn why I say it.

STOCKS ARE GIRLFRIENDS AND BONDS ARE BUDDIES

The real difference between stocks and bonds

Let's think about stocks and bonds in terms of a relationship.

Just like in a relationship, you are tied to the success/failure of a stock

Stocks are like your boyfriend/girlfriend or spouse. You are connected with them. Their success is your success. If they get a promotion, you celebrate and reap the rewards. If they come home and tell you they've been fired, that has real repercussions for you. If they want to take their savings and blow it in Vegas, you would try to talk them out of it because you not only have an interest in their well-being, but you also have a financial interest in their success and failure as well. If they win the Powerball lottery, you win the lottery. A stock is your significant other.

Relationships can be a bit rocky. From the highs of walking hand in hand on a Caribbean beach, to the lows of arguing, yelling, and even breakups, relationships give you the highest highs and the lowest lows. There is an intensity and volatility to relationships – or maybe it's just my relationships – in the same way that is true for stocks. They are volatile. They can produce great returns or make you go bankrupt.

Now let's look at a bond. A bond is like a friend. Do you care about your friend? Of course! You want them to succeed and do well. But on some level, if your buddy wants to blow some money in Vegas, as long as he can pay you back the money you lent him, you don't really care. If he hits the jackpot and wins millions, good on him. If he comes back broke, beaten up, and with an STD, that's too bad, but it's not going to ruin your day. Your friend's success or failures don't have much of an impact on your daily life. A bond is your friend.

There is also much less volatility in a friendship. Things are usually pretty stable. If you have a little tiff or get sick of your friend, you give it a few days and everything is back on track. There isn't the same level of intensity or volatility. The same is true for bonds.

Stocks are like a significant other. Stocks are a commitment. They represent a long-term interest in the success of a company. For better or for worse. For richer and for poorer.

Enough of this relationship talk! Let's get back to making cold hard cash. In the next lesson, you'll learn one popular way to do just that.

UH, WHAT'S
A MUTUAL FUND?

It may not be what you think…

You will hear about different types of investments, things like individual stocks or bonds, mutual funds, exchange traded funds, REITs, and even limited partnerships. They are all a slightly different, so it makes sense to have a little understanding of what these are and how they work.

Let's start at the beginning. What's an individual stock or bond? This one is pretty straightforward and something we covered in an earlier chapter. An individual stock is stock in a single company. For example, shares of Apple or shares of Ford or shares of Coca Cola. If you own 100 shares of Nike, you own, well, 100 shares of Nike. That's it. You have 100 shares of an individual company. The same thing is true of individual bonds. You can buy individual bonds for Nike, or Home Depot, or Chevron. Individual stocks or bonds are single investments into a single, and therefore individual, company.

Let's build on that.

About 100 years ago, someone came up with a different type of investment. Not a new asset class, like, "Hey! Let's invest in dandelions." They came up with a new way to invest. They created something called a mutual fund, and they are really popular even today. As an investor, you will almost certainly invest in a mutual fund if you haven't already.

All right, already! So what's a mutual fund?

Instead of investing in a single individual investment like a stock or bond, a mutual fund invests in a whole basket of them. When you buy a mutual fund, you are buying the whole enchilada, which means you own a piece of each of the investments in the basket.

A mutual fund is like a basket of investments

It's like those straight from the farm vegetable boxes you can buy. I did that once. I opened the box, and I didn't even recognize half the vegetables in it. Carrots, I knew. Corn, I recognized. I think I saw a couple of tomatoes. But the other stuff? Who knows? Too bad, though. I bought the box. I can't pick and choose only the vegetables I like and want. I get all of them.

Same is true with a mutual fund. You get everything.

And here is something many investors don't realize: a mutual fund is just the basket. It is the device or structure that holds stuff. Don't assume that if you own a mutual fund, the basket is filled with stocks.

It may be, but it could be filled with bonds instead. Or maybe a mixture of stocks and bonds. Maybe some real estate. Again, the mutual fund is just the basket. It tells you that this mutual fund you have owns some other things, but it doesn't tell you what those things are.

Does that make sense? Good. But our work isn't done. There's a new kid on the block that may just be better than a mutual fund. You'll learn what it is in the next lesson.

UH, WHAT'S AN EXCHANGE TRADED FUND (ETF)?

Fancy name for a basic (but important!) investment

Your *Get Money Smart* education would not be complete if we didn't talk briefly about this next type of investment.

Good news! In the last lesson, you learned not only about mutual funds, but you also learned about exchange traded funds, or ETFs, as they are called.

ETFs are a little different from mutual funds, but generally speaking, they do the same thing. They are just a basket that holds investments. Again, those investments could be stocks or bonds or whatever.

So if you hear someone talk about a mutual fund or ETF, you now know these are just the packaging that holds some underlying investments.

But they sound similar, don't they? So what makes an ETF different from a mutual fund? It comes down to taxes. Basically, you may be able to pay a lot less tax by owning an ETF instead of a mutual fund. Here's why. A mutual fund, remember, is a basket of holdings. Those holdings may go up or down in value throughout the year. If there are a lot of gains, then the mutual fund has to pass those gains on to the mutual fund owners. That would be you. That also means those gains will be taxable to you. But not so with an ETF. The pros say ETFs are more tax efficient.

Chances are your portfolio will have a mixture of both mutual funds and ETFs, so it's important to understand a bit about both.

HOW THE STOCK MARKET WORKS

How the Stock Market Is like Tinder

Are you familiar with the dating app Tinder? It lets you view photos of people and slide their photo left or right, depending on if you like them or not.

So how is the stock market like Tinder?

Seriously though, how is the stock market like Tinder?

For both, you have a large group of people coming together and they are all evaluating a limited number of things. On Tinder, there are a limited number of photos that people are clamoring over. In the stock market, there are a limited number of stocks available to investors. They are both beauty pageants.

The stock market is just like any market. It's a place where people can come together to buy and sell things. In this case, it is shares of stock. Maybe you inherited some stock and now you want to sell it. Well, that's what the stock market is all about. It's the place to go where people who want to sell shares hook up with people who want to buy shares.

So if you are a buyer, you go there and you can buy shares of stock. If you are a seller, you go there and you can sell your shares of stock. If a lot of people want the same stock, the price goes up. If everyone wants to sell the same stock, the price goes down. It's really nothing more than connecting buyers with sellers.

A common misconception is that when you buy shares of stock, you are buying them directly from the company. For example, when

I buy Apple stock, the thought is I'm buying them from Apple, the company. Not so. I'm actually buying them from some other person. For example, when I buy 10 shares of Apple stock, there is someone else out there who has sold 10 shares of Apple stock.

There is also a bond market, an options market, a futures market, a commodities market, etc. They all work the same. They simply connect buyers with sellers.

In the next lesson, you'll hear the sweetest words in the English language: I love you. No, just kidding. The sweetest words in the English language are, "The market was up today." You'll also get a quick lesson on what the heck this really means.

WHAT DO THEY MEAN WHEN THEY SAY THE "MARKET WAS UP TODAY"?

Impress your friends with your financial knowledge

You might hear it on the radio, in a news broadcast, or read it online. The stock market used to be this esoteric industry that only a few people were a part of and even fewer knew anything about. But then, as more and more of the public became investors through their 401(k)s, they started to take more of an interest in it. Now, investing and the stock market is like the Super Bowl every Monday through Friday. We have entire TV networks that do nothing but talk about the stock market. We have radio programs, books, magazines, and websites dedicated to all things investing. The stock market has become sexy.

Up where? What does it all mean???

You'll often hear reports about the market saying it was up today or it was down today, or that it was up and then down today. It was down and then up today. You get the point. Most of this is just nonsense chatter. Does it really matter what happens in the stock market in a single day? Usually, not so much.

But, it is important to at least know what the heck they mean by *the stock market was up or down.*

The stock market is the place buyers and sellers come together, but it is also the term used to describe how not just one stock is doing but how a lot of stocks are doing. A single stock is ownership in a single company, like Tesla, Johnson & Johnson, or ExxonMobil. The stock market is looking at how they all did today. Were they up or down?

A lot of times, when you hear about the stock market, they are referring to something called the Dow or the Dow Jones Industrial Average. This is 30 big U.S. companies such as AT&T, Wal-Mart, American Express, Nike, and Disney. On any given day, these 30 stocks go up or down. Take all 30 of them together, and you can determine if the Dow is up or down that day. But there are thousands of stocks that trade on the stock market each day, so how can these 30 represent "the stock market"? Well, they can't really. That's why most astute investors disregard the Dow and focus instead on the S&P 500.

This is the same sort of thing as with the Dow, but instead of a collection of only 30 companies, the S&P 500 is made up of 500 companies.

So you can see how the S&P 500 gets you a much better idea of how the overall market did.

The next time you hear, "The market was down today," see if they mention the Dow or the S&P 500. And while you're listening, you just might hear something about a bull or a bear. Strange, I know. But in the next lesson, you'll get the inside scoop on what a bull and a bear have to do with investing.

WHAT DO THEY MEAN WHEN THEY TALK ABOUT BULLS AND BEARS?

It's like a zoo around here

Bull markets go up, while bear markets go down

Okay, so what in the world are they talking about when they call the stock market a bull or a bear?

You'll hear this a lot, so you should know what it means.

A bull market is a stock market going up in value, and not just for the day, but over an extended period of time – months or even years. You might hear that someone is "bullish" on the market or "bullish" on a particular investment. It just means they are optimistic it will go up.

A bear market is just the opposite. It is a stock market that is going down in value. Again, just because the market goes down today doesn't mean we have a bear market. If the market has been going down over the past several months or years, we could call it a bear market. You may also hear that an investor is "bearish" on the market or on a particular investment. This just means they are pessimistic and think the market or investment will go down in value.

Here's a quick trick to help you remember these. Think about how each of these animals strike their prey. A bull thrusts its horns upward and a bear uses its paws to strike down. Get it? Bull horn up and bear claw down?

Pop quiz. If you are bullish on Amazon stock, do you buy it or sell it?

If you are bullish, you think the stock will go up, so you'd want to buy it now.

If you are bearish on Amazon stock, do you buy it or sell it?

If you are bearish, you think the stock will go down, so you'd want to sell it now.

The next lesson is a fun one, and it might just help if you're ever a contestant on Jeopardy.

WHY IS IT CALLED WALL STREET?

The only geography lesson in the book

Yes, it's actually a street

You may hear news commentators say, "The action on Wall Street today was strong, blah, blah, blah." What do they mean by *Wall Street*?

Wall Street refers to the financial and investment community. In fact, there was a movie way back in the 1980s called *Wall Street,* and it was about the stock market (side note: if you ever watch this movie, there is a scene with a cell phone literally the size of a shoebox). Wall Street is synonymous with investing.

But why is it called Wall Street? Simple: there is a financial district in New York and there is actually a street in the southern part of Manhattan called "Wall Street." If you're ever in New York, you should check it out. Guess what's on this street? The New York Stock Exchange. This is the heart of investing, where most people used to buy and sell stocks. So now, anything related to investing or finances is called Wall Street.

UH, WHAT'S AN INDEX?

All about apples . . . the fruit; not the company

How will you know how your harvest is doing?

Imagine you are an apple farmer, and you have a bunch of acres and thousands of apple trees. Side note, have you had a Honeycrisp apple?! These things are amazing. I should know; I'm from Washington State, the land of angst-filled musicians, rain, and apples.

In your apple orchard, you have different types of apple trees and millions of apples. You've got a lot riding on this harvest. If they turn out sweet and crisp, you will make a lot of money. If they are a bit mushy, you've got problems. But how can you know? Well, I suppose you could pick every apple and take a bite of each one to see if it's a good apple. But that's not going to work too well.

What else could you do? You could pick an apple from each different type of apple tree in your orchard. You'd pick some apples from your Honeycrisp trees and some apples from your Granny Smith trees, etc. You're basically taking a sample from each tree so you have a good indication of how each type of apple is doing. It's quick and it gives you a pretty good idea of how all the apples are doing.

That's what a stock index is. It's a basket of stocks. For example, the Dow Jones Industrial Average is an index. It only has 30 stocks in it, and it tries to represent how large companies in the U.S. are doing. There are thousands of large U.S. companies, but the Dow has just 30, and these 30 give us an idea of how they are all doing.

An index is just a collection of investments. There are many indexes out there that contain almost any type of investment you could imagine. There's an index of oil companies, small Russian companies, Chinese technology companies, high yield bonds, municipal bonds, and on and on.

This way, you can look at the different parts of the market and get a good idea how each has done. You can quickly look at an index and see that bonds from emerging markets are not doing well, but restaurant company stocks in the U.S. are doing great.

So that's one reason an index is important, but as you'll see later, there's a much more important reason – a game-changing important reason.

ACTIVE VS. PASSIVE INVESTING

A tale of two brothers

Cornelius, the Type A, analytical active investor

Here's a little story. It's a story of two seemingly different brothers who share a common job.

Cornelius was a rather astute and precocious child. He was a hard worker. Very analytical and Type A. He had to be right, so he spent hours and hours in his room researching and learning. He got a perfect score on his SAT and went on to get an MBA in finance and statistics. Cornelius started an investment company – he started a mutual fund where he focused on discovering, analyzing, and investing in large cap U.S. companies. He spent hours digging through their financials and would crisscross the country, meeting with the executives of the companies he was thinking about investing in. He had detailed spreadsheets and forecasts of the companies, their competitors, and the economy. He spent every waking minute buying companies he thought would do well and selling companies if he thought they would no longer do well. Every year, his mutual fund performance would be compared to other mutual funds and would be compared to a similar index. In his case, the index would be other large cap U.S. stocks. His fund would be scrutinized, and he worked more and more hours to do better than the other mutual funds.

He had a whole staff of other analysts who did the same thing he did. They would look at 100 companies and select one or two to invest in. You could say Cornelius was quite active in his approach – always analyzing and studying, and buying and selling.

His brother, Bodhi, was not quite as intense. Bodhi was more interested in surfing (you get extra credit if you can tell me the '90s movie with a surfer named Bodhi!). Sure, he liked to make money, but he also like to hang ten.

Bodhi saw the success of his brother, so he asked Cornelius for a job.

Bodhi, the laidback passive investor

"You must be joking!" Cornelius retorted. "I would never hire you. You couldn't even get your GED."

Rejected and dejected, Bodhi decided to start his own mutual fund. He saw how hard his brother worked and the long hours he put in. Bodhi thought, "Man, if I work like him, dude, I'll never catch another wave in my life. That's bogus." So, he decided his mutual fund would be a little different.

Instead of doing all that research, analysis, and flying all over the country trying to find the best companies, he would skip all that. Instead, he went in on January 2 (the market is closed for New Year's Day) and simply looked at what an index with large cap U.S. companies had in it (all indexes will list what investments are in the index). He then bought those companies for his mutual fund. Then the next January 2, he would compare what he owned versus the index. Maybe the index replaced some of their investments with others. No problem. Bodhi would sell those and buy the new investments. It took him about 20 minutes every January 2. The rest of the year, he surfed.

Now, I don't want to call Bodhi lazy. You might call him passive. He wasn't trying to do all kinds of research and buy and sell throughout the year, month, or day. He just stuck with whatever investments were part of the index.

Cornelius was an active manager. In fact, his style of investing is called "active management," for pretty obvious reasons. He was very active. He was trying to beat the market or the index.

Bodhi wasn't trying to beat the market; he was trying to be the market. His approach was passive. His style of investing is called "passive management." It's a bit like saying "jumbo shrimp," though. It's passive, but can you really call it "management"? He didn't do much at all. There was little management, but whatever. That's what his style of investing is called. It's also referred to as index investing. Get it? He's investing in an index.

So these are two *very* different styles. Why is it important to know about them?

It can get pretty expensive to hire all of those analysts and travel all over the country. Active investment managers are usually more expensive as a result. Compare that to the passive index investing approach. Very little overhead. Very few expenses.

Yes, but won't Cornelius get a much better return because he's doing all that research and analysis? Well, you'd think so and you'd hope so. And that's definitely the promise of using an active manager. But, sadly, that's not always the case.

And in the next lesson, you'll find out why.

30

WHICH STYLE DOES BETTER? ACTIVE OR PASSIVE INVESTING?

You might be shocked at this...

About 86% of active large cap managers beat their index in 2014. Only 86%. That means 14% of these higher cost ADHD OCD managers didn't even do as well as their index.

Oops, wait! I made a tiny mistake. I didn't mean to suggest that only 86% of active managers beat their index. I have to be careful around here. I could get sued for libel. Let me retract that.

Only 14% Active Managers Beat Index

— — Average Index Return — —

86%

Active Managers Did Worse Than Index!

You'll be fine just sticking with a passive investment manager

It turns out 86% is the correct number, but the truth is, 86% of active managers *failed* to beat their index. Yeah, you heard me. A total of 86% of these active managers did worse than the index. All those airplane meals and Excel spreadsheets and you do worse?! Yup. And it's not like 2014 was some weird aberration.

So you'd probably be better off investing with the surfer-hippie-couldn't-even-pass-the-GED Bodhi than an active manager.

This is the big debate in the investment world. Active managers say, "We can beat the market," and then you have reality saying, "No, most of you can't and don't."

As an investor, there may be some circumstances where you will want to have active managers, but for the bulk of your portfolio (or even all of it!), you can't go wrong with a lazy, uh, I mean, a passive index approach.

31

SALES, EXPENSES, PROFITS, OH MY!

Common misunderstood financial terms

Here's a quick lesson for you. It's surprising how few people really understand what you're about to learn.

What are sales? Well, sales can also be called gross revenue, gross sales, gross receipts, or total sales. Whatever you want to call it, sales are the total value of all products and services a company generates in a month, quarter, or year.

Let's look at your local car dealership. Maybe in a given quarter they sell a bunch of cars. They sell 100 cars, each worth $40,000, and the total amount of money they collect is $4 million. Wow! $4 million! They buy a cake and they celebrate. They give each other high fives. That's total sales.

But then some guy in accounting raises his hand and says, "I hate to ruin the party, but we had to pay for those cars we just sold." Turns out, they bought those cars for $3.5 million. That's an expense. They also had to pay their employees. And the electric bill. And rent on the lot. And don't forget about the cake they just bought. These are all expenses. The accounting guy does some calculations and says, "Our total expenses for everything add up to $3.8 million."

Don't be tricked into ignoring expenses

And then they start celebrating again because their profit, which is their total sales minus their expenses, turns out to be $200,000.

That's sales, expenses, and profit.

My clients get pitched on a lot of private companies and investments. The first thing I do when I review these pitches is look at the numbers usually hidden in the back of the packet. The pitch in big bold letters often focuses on the total sales. "Look at us! We sold $2 million last year!" Okay, and what were your expenses? $3 million? Oh! That hurts.

WHY A STOCK
GOES UP AND DOWN

All about company earnings

Why does the stock market go up and down?

Well, the stock market has been likened to a teenage girl because of its erratic moods and volatility. But that's not really a fair thing to say about teenage girls. Their mood swings are not as bad as the stock market.

So what causes this up and down rollercoaster ride?

Short-term movements of individual stocks or the market as a whole can't really be described with much certainty, so what happens hour by hour or day by day is hard to pinpoint.

But in the longer-term, it becomes a bit easier to understand and explain. It's like a Monet painting. Up close, everything is an indecipherable mess. Nothing seems to make sense. But with distance and time, it all becomes much clearer.

One of the real drivers of the market occurs four times a year when companies report their quarterly earnings.

Forget about investing for a second. Instead, imagine if every three months your boyfriend, girlfriend, spouse, or mistress sat you down and then proceeded to provide you with a report of everything you did over the previous three months – the flowers you bought her, the birthday you forgot, and the split-second glance at the pretty woman in the checkout line. Yes, she took notes of everything you did and then assigned you a grade. This would be brutal.

Welcome to quarterly earnings. Every three months, public companies report on how they did over the previous quarter. How much

Earnings reports let investors know how companies are doing

stuff they sold, what their expenses were, etc. It's a full-blown detailed report of practically everything that happened.

And guess who is interested in reading this report? Everyone! If you are invested in the company, you want to know how the company did. There will be people who focus on a particular company or industry whose job it is to really become experts at the companies they follow. These people are called analysts. If an analyst follows Wal-Mart or the retail industry around Christmas, she doesn't go to the shopping mall to pick up presents. Nope. She goes there to see if the parking lot is full and to count the people going into or out of stores. These analysts then come up with how much money they predict the company will make in a quarter. These are called earnings predictions. That is, they are trying to predict what the company will earn in the future.

For example, if an analyst says a company will make $2 billion in a quarter but the company actually earns $3 billion, that surprise could really get people interested in the stock, and you might see a lot of people buying shares. This could drive the stock up. On the other hand, if the company reports they only made $1 billion, that could scare a lot of investors and they might start selling. This could drive down the price.

You might hear that a company "missed earnings." This just means a bunch of analysts thought they'd earn so much, but the company actually earned less. On the flipside, you could hear a company "beat earnings," which means they did better than what investors and analysts thought they'd do.

Earnings can really move the price of a stock each quarter, and over time, it is often how well the company does selling whatever it sells that drives the price of the stock. If the company is selling more, hiring employees, expanding to new cities and countries, and cutting expenses, these are all things that are positive for the company and could increase the company's earnings and get investors excited.

The takeaway? Companies let investors know how they did every three months (or four times a year). These are called earnings reports. The investors look at these very closely and will often respond by buying or selling based on how the company did and by how the company says it thinks it will do going forward.

WHAT ARE ASSET CLASSES?

The building blocks of investing

As an investor, you're bound to hear a lot about asset classes. This is one of those key areas in which you'll want some level of understanding. In other words, you would definitely *not* be money smart if you didn't know about asset classes.

So let's jump in.

An asset class is just a fancy phrase for investments that are similar to each other. This group of investments has similar characteristics and behaves in a similar way. As a comparison, think about all the different kinds of vehicles that are available. Everything from a Corvette and a Land Rover to a Harley motorcycle to a Prius. These are all very different, but could you start to categorize all of the vehicles into a few different groups? Sure you could. You could put the Corvette with the Porsche and the Ferrari. We'd label these sports cars. We could then group the Land Rover with the Ford Explorer and the Suburban. These would be SUVs. We'd group the minivans together. Maybe we'd put the luxury cars into their own group. You get the point. We started out with lots of different individual vehicles, but we could group them together into similar categories.

Asset classes are the same thing when it comes to investing. There are four main groups, or asset classes, for investors. These are stocks, bonds, cash, and real estate. Sure, there are investments that don't neatly fit into these categories, but this encompasses most of what you'll come across.

That's it. Just stocks, bonds, cash, and real estate. We humans love to put things into boxes because it's so helpful. If your friend texts you that he just bought a new SUV, you have a pretty good idea of what he has. Instead, if he says he just bought a new sports car, again, you can infer a lot from just knowing the category.

Just like you can tell a lot about the categories of cars, the same holds up with investment asset classes.

How is this helpful in the real world? Let's look at a few different scenarios:

	Stock Happy	Bond Happy	Cash Happy
Stocks:	100%	0%	0%
Bonds:	0%	100%	0%
Cash:	0%	0%	100%

Now let's say the stock market has a great year and goes up 25%. How is Stock Happy's portfolio going to do? Awesome! Bond Happy? Okay. Cash Happy? Not very good.

Now let's say the stock market has a bad year and goes down 25%. How is Stock Happy's portfolio going to do? Lousy. Bond Happy? Good! Cash Happy? Great!

Even though you don't know anything about the actual investments – the actual stocks that Stock Happy owned or the types of bonds that Bond Happy has – you can quickly and accurately tell how well they did in each of these scenarios.

This is why understanding asset classes is so important as an investor.

The four main asset classes for investors

Are there other asset classes? The short answer is yes. You can start with the four main asset classes: stocks, bonds, cash, and real estate, and then you can get even fancier by categorizing these into sub-asset classes, but that's for another time.

Here's a quiz for you. What's wrong with this statement: "My asset allocation is 60% mutual funds, 40% ETFs." Come on. Make me proud.

Well, did you notice anything fishy about that statement? We know the main asset classes are stocks, bonds, cash, and real estate.

Is a mutual fund an asset class? Is an ETF an asset class? No! A mutual fund could be entirely invested in anything. All stocks. Or maybe all bonds. Your asset allocation is *not* mutual funds and ETFs. You would have to determine what your mutual funds and ETFs are invested in to really know what your asset allocation is.

It's like saying, "I'm having a plate and a bowl for dinner." Huh? Those are just the devices that hold your food. They are meaningless unless you know what's in your bowl or on your plate. Does that make sense?

Okay. I need to take a break. All this talk of food and I'm starting to get hungry.

In the next few chapters you will learn more about stocks, bonds, and real estate.

34

DIGGING DEEPER INTO STOCKS: PART 1

Not all stocks are created equally…

We've spent a lot of time on stocks because, as an investor, it will be one of the main types of investments in your portfolio. And I've said that stocks are a main asset class, which means stocks generally share many characteristics and tend to behave similarly.

And all of that is absolutely true. But it's also like saying all fruit is the same. Sure, looking at all foods, you know if two things are classified as fruit they're going to look and taste much more similar to each other than these other two foods categorized as meat. So, it's important to know if this is fruit or if this is meat. That's a valuable bit of information, especially if you're a vegetarian.

But, wow! There are so many different kinds of fruit. Sure, they share similar characteristics, but come on. You have oranges and grapefruit and tangerines over here, and then you have cantaloupe, honeydew, and watermelons over there. All fruit, yes. But there are big differences between an orange and a watermelon, no?

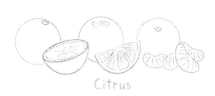

Citrus

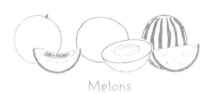

Melons

Sub-categories, or sub-asset classes, share similar characteristics

This is why we break our fruit down into smaller sub-categories, such as citrus and melons. We don't just arbitrarily do this. Fruits within each of these sub-categories have similar characteristics. There's a reason we group oranges, lemons, and limes together.

Back to stocks! Generally, stocks have similar characteristics.

Got it. Check. Now let's break them down further into sub-categories, or what we call sub-asset classes.

But where do we begin?! I don't know. I mean, you have all these different types of companies all over the world. How are we supposed to start? Hmm, well, I guess we could do it first by geography. If we did that, we'd have U.S. companies in one category and then stock from companies not in the U.S. in an international category. That works. But there's a big difference between a company headquartered in Switzerland and a company in Cambodia. Nothing against Cambodia – I've been several times and it's a wonderful country with wonderful people. Switzerland has a stable and big economy and government. Cambodia is not as established and their economy is not as big or stable. If there was only a way we could distinguish between the more developed countries and those countries that are more emerging. It would be helpful to know if I'm investing in one of these developed international countries or in one of the not quite as developed but emerging countries. Eureka! I've got it. We could call them Developed and Emerging.

So, for stocks, we now have three sub-asset classes: U.S., developed international, and emerging international. Again, these are not arbitrary categories. Each of these sub-asset classes has similar characteristics. We don't just randomly make up these categories; we do it with a purpose. We want to be able to understand how our portfolio might perform under different conditions. It's helpful if we know we have 100% to U.S. stocks compared to 100% to emerging market stocks. That is a meaningful distinction.

But we can slice and dice stocks up even more than in a game of *Fruit Ninja*. More in the next lesson.

35

DIGGING DEEPER INTO STOCKS: PART 2

Here's another way to look at stocks...

In the last lesson, you learned that geography is an important distinction. Are there are any categories that might be important? Let's look at U.S. stocks. We know these are different and may perform differently from developed international stocks and emerging market stocks. But do you think there is much of a difference between a company such as Wal-Mart and, I don't know, maybe the Seattle company, Bill the Butcher, Inc.? Bill the who? Exactly. But this is a real company. I couldn't make this up even if I wanted.

So Wal-Mart is ginormous and has revenue of nearly $500 billion a year, and our buddy Bill has revenue of less than $2 million a year.

Yes, they are both in the United States and that's helpful to know, but come on. Huge difference between these two companies. One is large and the other small. Bingo. That's another way we can categorize stocks: by how large they are.

If you really want to be clever, the size of the company is not technically determined by their sales, but by their market cap instead. Market cap is short for market capitalization. It sounds ominous, but it's really simple to understand. You just look at the number of total shares a company has and you multiply it by the price of one share. So what you get is the dollar amount it would take if you wanted to buy the whole company. For example, a company has 100 total shares and the stock price for one share is $5; that means you could buy up all 100 shares of the stock and own the company with $500.

Just for fun, how much do you think the market cap of Wal-Mart is? About $250 billion. And Billy the Butcher? About $60,000.

So, yes, one company is bigger than the other, but as an investor, how is this helpful? Think of it this way. A large company has most likely been around much longer. They probably have lots of customers, cash, and profits. They may have equipment and infrastructure. Because they are so big, they may be able to borrow money a little easier. If there is suddenly a drop in the economy and people are not spending money and buying things, will a big company like Wal-Mart be affected? Absolutely. But chances are, they are so big and have such resources that they could ride out any downturn. In fact, because they are so big, they could lower prices to attract more clients. It might cost them in profits in the short-term, but they might generate a loyal following and customers even after the economy picks back up.

Small companies have more growth potential than larger, more mature ones

What about butcher boy? It's a much different story. They are small. They don't have the same amount of cash or ability to borrow. If there is a downturn, and they lose a few customers, that could drastically affect their ability to pay their rent and keep going as a company. There's much more risk with a small company, but there may be a lot more growth potential as well. A large company has already done much of their growing. They are mature. But get a company when it's small and you could see huge growth over the years. Think about it. Wal-Mart was once a small company, and now it's worth nearly a quarter of a trillion dollars!

One is not better or worse than the other. The point is that they behave differently from one another but similarly with other stocks in their sub-asset class. Meaning, most really small companies will face the same challenges in a downturn, yet they may also have greater potential for growth.

It's important to know if you have a portfolio that consists of small company stocks, like Bill the Butcher, or big company stocks, like Wal-Mart.

So those are the main ways to categorize stocks: by geography – U.S., developed, or emerging markets – and by size – small, mid-sized, or large.

This is good stuff, if I do say so myself. Are you ready for the not so pop quiz I'm warning you about in the next lesson? It counts for 25% of your final grade.

36

DIGGING DEEPER
INTO STOCKS: POP QUIZ

Can you pass this quiz?

Knowing what you know right now, what would be the most volatile and potentially risky asset class of these: large U.S. or small U.S.? Yes, small U.S. because the smaller the company is, the more risky it usually is.

Okay, a little harder now. Large developed or large emerging market? Here, both are large, so you have to look at where they are. Developed are usually more stable and secure, and emerging markets are less stable, so the answer would be large emerging market.

Okay, last one. Large U.S. or small emerging market? Definitely small emerging market, because you have small companies in less stable countries.

Are there other ways to chop up different stocks into various categories? Yes. For example, if you had to group these companies into two groups, *Google, Bank of America, Microsoft, Wells Fargo, Facebook, and Visa*, how would you do it? They all are big. They are all U.S. companies. What if you looked at what industry they were in? You have Google, Microsoft, and Facebook. They all seem to be technology related. And then you have Bank of America, Wells Fargo, and Visa. They all seem to be finance related. And this is certainly another way to categorize investments – by industry.

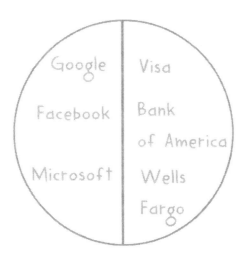

Your asset allocation provides insight on how your portfolio might perform and the amount of risk you're taking

Again, why would we do this? Not just for the fun of it. It provides meaningful information to us as investors. We want to know if most of our portfolio is invested in technology stocks versus financial stocks, because these industries are very different and perform differently. It's possible for financial stocks to do really well, while most technology companies don't do well. Or vice versa.

We look at asset classes, sub-asset classes, and industries because it provides helpful information and insight on our portfolio, how it might perform, and the amount of risk we are taking.

37

DIGGING DEEPER INTO BONDS

Bonds don't have to be boring...

Just like you can split up stocks into different categories, we can do the same thing with bonds. And by doing this, it can tell us a great deal about our investments and how we are invested.

Here are the main sub-asset classes when it comes to bonds:

Geography	Issuer	Length of Loan	Credit Score
U.S.	Government	Long	Excellent
Developed	Municipality	Mid	Okay
Emerging	Corporation	Short	Bad

Who Borrows?

Municipalities

Governments

Corporations

Who is issuing the bond?

Good news! You already have the geography types down. U.S. just means the bonds are from the U.S. Developed means bonds are from other countries outside the U.S., but they are more developed like the U.S., countries such as Canada, France, Japan, England, and Australia. Then you have emerging markets. These are also countries outside the U.S., but are not quite as developed, such as Brazil, India, Thailand, and Turkey.

But let's look at the Issuer category. What does that mean, Issuer? It means who you are lending the money to. That is, who is borrowing the money by issuing a bond? Well, there are a lot of different groups out there that would love to borrow money from you. Here are the big three that issue bonds: Governments, Corporations, and Municipalities.

People are often surprised that governments borrow money, but it's true! They borrow big time! The U.S. government borrows a boatload of money all the time. How much do we owe? Take a guess. $1 million? $100 million? Not even close. We owe $18 trillion!

So do governments borrow money? Well, if you consider $18 trillion to be money, then sure, I would say they do. And it's not just the U.S. government; countries around the world borrow, too. But why? The short answer is they need the money. It costs a lot of money to have a military, to pay for disaster relief, IRS employees, and the FBI.

But one day, a group of people got envious of all this borrowing. They wanted to borrow money, too, but they were just a little city. They weren't a big country. No problem! States and cities, also called municipalities, can borrow as well. Yes, that includes you, Los Angeles, Texas, and Chicago, but also the little guys out there, such as Billings, Montana; Chattanooga, Tennessee; and Rhode Island. They can all issue bonds and borrow money. But again, why would they want to borrow? Lots of reasons. They may want to build a new bridge or road. They may want to construct a new city hall or football stadium.

And then finally, we can't forget the last of the big three, corporations. That is, companies. They borrow a lot of money, too. Companies like Wal-Mart, Microsoft, and Yum Brands, the company that owns KFC, Pizza Hut, and Taco Bell.

Who cares? Why are we always trying to put things into different boxes? Because we can understand a great deal about a bond just by knowing if it is a government, municipality, or corporation that issues it.

The last two categories, you understand. The length of the loan, also called the term, is when you will get back the money you lend, and it's either a long time or a short time from now. Then you have credit score, or what we call credit quality. What is the likelihood you are going to get your money back?

That's it. That's how you can split up and think about different types bonds.

38

DO BONDS
HAVE CREDIT SCORES?

Would you loan me money?

A credit quality of
"A" would be better

Can I borrow $10,000?

What do you need to know to make a good decision?

Let's say we're friends, so you don't want to charge me any interest, but is there anything more you'd want to know?

Well, I guess you'd need to know how long I want to borrow it for. Is it for a month or ten years? That might affect your decision to lend it to me.

What else? You'd probably size me up and try to figure out if I'd be able to pay you back. Do I have a secure job? Have I borrowed money from you in the past and paid it back? Do I owe a bunch of people money? Heck, a good idea might be to get my credit score. This number would tell you how responsible I am with loans. A high credit score means I have my stuff together. A low credit score means I've had some problems in the past – maybe I filed for bankruptcy, have some late payments, or just owe too many people too much.

Guess what? The questions you'd have for me if I wanted to borrow money are the same questions you'd have if you buy a bond. Again, a bond is just a promise for someone to pay you back, just like a friend borrowing money from you.

But, of course, we have a few fancy terms for you to be aware of.

The length of the loan is simply called the term. This can be long-term, which is any loan or bond 10 years or more. Then there's mid-term, which is usually 3 to 10 years. And then short-term, which is under 3 years.

Now, instead of credit score, we say credit quality. It means the same thing, though. They even have a grading system from "A" all the way down to "D." So, as you can imagine, a credit quality of "A" means this is a borrower that has great credit. Chances are you are going to get your money back. A credit quality of "C" means this borrower is pretty shaky. You might not get your money back.

So if you might not get your money back, why would you ever do it? There's a million-dollar reason that you'll learn in the next chapter.

39

WHY WOULD I EVER LEND MONEY TO A SHADY FRIEND?

How to loan money to a deadbeat friend

Let's say you have a couple of friends and they each want to borrow money from you. One of them has a great job, and the other always seems to have some kind of issue – he's always broke, getting fired, and sleeping on friends' couches because he can't pay rent. And trust me, we *all* have a friend like that.

But here they are. They both want to borrow $1,000 from you. It's probably an easy decision to lend money to your responsible friend, but why would you ever lend money to your deadbeat friend?

Because you want to make money! Here's how it works.

In the last lesson, you learned about bonds and credit scores, or what we call credit quality. A good credit quality means there is a good chance you will get your money back. A bad credit quality means there is a good chance you won't get your money back.

There are bonds from companies just like your deadbeat friend. There are companies that might not make a lot of money and might owe a lot of people a lot of money. Bottom line, it's a company that may struggle to pay you back if anything goes wrong in their business.

Okay, so why buy their bond? Why give a company (or a friend) your hard-earned money when there is a higher chance that they may not be able to pay you back?

What if I said that deadbeat company would pay you more interest? A lot more interest? A high amount of interest? This is exactly what happens.

You have two companies. One big, stable company like Disney that issues bonds – that is, wants to borrow money from investors.

Everyone knows Disney and knows it's a big company with lots of cash that will almost definitely pay back the money they borrow. I mean, what are the chances Disney is going to go out of business?

Now, over here, you have Bill the Butcher, Inc. again. Tiny company. Not very much in sales. Very little cash on hand. Lots of debt.

They each want to borrow $1,000 and you lend it to both of them. Why? What would have caused you to lend money to Bill the Butcher? What in the name of all that is good would have possessed you to do this? Why not just loan the full $2,000 to Disney?

It's the one thing that causes most people to do most things: cold hard cash in the form of interest.

Both bonds from each company are going to pay interest, but which company will have to pay more interest to lure investors to loan them money?

Will it be Mickey? Come on! This is Disney we're talking about. They know they are Disney. They know we know they are Disney. They know they have a great credit quality. If they want to borrow $1,000, they don't need to entice people by paying a lot of interest. They might pay just 5% interest on their bond.

Fair enough. So if you have a big stable company like Disney willing to pay 5% interest, what kind of interest rate will Billy have to pay? 4%? Of course not! It has to be higher. Much higher. I mean a lot, lot, lot higher. Probably 10% or maybe 12%. Now that's a high interest rate. In the financial world, this is called a high yield bond. Yield just means interest rate. So high yield bonds are those that pay a high interest rate. Why pay a high interest rate? Because no one would lend them money by buying their bonds if they didn't pay a high interest rate.

The takeaway is that it might make sense to lend money to companies that don't have great credit because you will get a much higher interest rate. High yield bonds have high interest rates and a higher chance you won't get your money back.

40

INVESTING IN REAL ESTATE: RAW VS. DEVELOPED

So You Wanna Be a Real Estate Tycoon?

"Buy land, they're not making anymore!" That little morsel was from one of my favorite authors, Mark Twain. It's also the rallying cry of every real estate agent and would-be real estate investor.

But before you jump in and start buying real estate, let's get you money smart.

Raw Land

For Sale

The riskier choice

Developed Land

For Sale

A safer bet

There are many different kinds of real estate, but just like stocks and bonds, we can break things down a bit further.

One of the most important ways to think about real estate is by putting it into one of two camps. In this camp, you have undeveloped land. What does that mean? It just means there is land but no manmade structures on the land. This is also called "raw" land. Drive out to the middle of the desert or forest, and this is raw, undeveloped land. Drive down the block and if you see an empty plot of land with nothing on it, that, my friend, is raw land.

The other camp over here is developed land. This has some kind of manmade structure on it – maybe a house, an apartment building, a strip mall, a Chuck E. Cheese, or a parking lot. All of these are things that were constructed and put on the raw land.

If you think about it, all land was raw land at one point. Times Square in NYC was once just raw land until they paved it over and put up buildings.

As an investor, you may get pitched on a real estate investment. Sometimes the pitch is to buy raw land and then build something on it, and other times, it is to buy an apartment or building that is already built. There are huge differences between these two camps, between raw land and developed. There is much greater risk with raw land, because you first have to build something. With developed real estate, that something, whatever it is, is already built. In fact, there may already be a business there with renters who can pay you money. With raw land, it may take years to build whatever it is they want to build. There are no renters yet, so you could go a long time without getting any money back. And let's say you buy the raw land, and the idea is to put up an office building. Okay, but once the building is done, you then have to get businesses to move into the new office building. It could take months or years before the office building you just built is full. Again, more risk.

So why would anyone invest in raw land? We come back to the driving force that explains why investors do anything: cash, Benjamins, bills, bread, greenbacks, bones, moola, or clams. Investors invest in raw land because while there is greater risk, there is also greater potential returns. In other words, they can make more money developing raw land.

But, again, as an investor, it's helpful to know what you're getting into. Invest in raw land and you might not see a dime for several years. Invest in developed land, and you could start getting money back in less than a month.

Okay, how else can we think about real estate other than undeveloped/raw and developed? In the next lesson, I'll show you.

41

HOW TO INVEST IN REAL ESTATE

Learn about the three different types

In the last chapter, you learned about the difference between raw and undeveloped real estate compared to developed real estate. As a reminder, undeveloped real estate means it's just land. No one has built anything on it yet. Developed means there is something there. Maybe a house, an apartment building, or a parking lot. Something.

How else can you think about real estate? How about by type? Absolutely. There are three main types of real estate: Residential, Commercial, and Industrial.

Residential	Commercial	Industrial
Single Family	Offices	Warehousing
Multi-Family	Retail	Manufacturing

These are the three main categories, but there are certainly others, which are often hybrids of these. For example, think about a hotel. Well, it's residential in that people sleep there, but it's also commercial. Or think about self-storage – you know, those places where you can keep all the junk that doesn't fit in your home? It has similarities to commercial but also a bit of industrial.

Each type of real estate has different characteristics, and they are going to perform differently. Think about owning a single family house and renting it. You'll get a monthly check in the mail, but you may also get a call at 3am that there is a plumbing issue. Compare that to a large office building. More work? Less work? Each is different.

Up next? I will share the Holy Grail of investing with you. Two words that are at the heart of investing. If you don't know what they are, you will soon.

WHAT IS ASSET ALLOCATION?

The fundamentals of investing

Asset allocation. The two words you'll hear on Wall Street more than "big" and "bonuses."

As an investor, asset allocation is one of those things you'll want to know something about.

The good news is that you already know a lot about it!

What is an asset class? Well, you may recall that the main asset classes are stocks, bonds, cash, and real estate. And sure, you learned about sub-asset classes, such as U.S. versus emerging markets, and small companies versus large companies, or long-term bonds versus short-term bonds. We know there are many ways we can slice this up into different categories.

But what about the allocation part? Allocation basically means how things are divided up. Therefore, asset allocation is simply looking at your investments and answering these two questions:

1.   What asset classes do I own?

2.   How much of each asset class do I own?

That's it. Do I own stocks? Yes. Okay, how much do I own? Do I own bonds? Yes. Okay, how much? Do I own cash? Yes. Okay, how much? Do I own real estate? No. Okay.

To make things easier, we look at what percentage of our total portfolio we own. We don't usually say, "I own $52,456.43 in small cap emerging market stocks," which doesn't really mean that much. Is that a lot to own of small cap emerging market stocks, an asset class that is fairly risky? Uh, well, it's hard to say.

Instead, it's more meaningful to think about what percent of your total portfolio this asset is, rather than the actual dollar amount you own. So, maybe that $52,456.43 you have invested in small cap emerging market stocks is 3% of your total investment portfolio. You know small cap emerging market stocks are pretty risky, but it looks like it only represents 3% of your total portfolio. That's not too risky or crazy. But what if that $52,456.43 represented 96% of your portfolio? Holy cow! Pump the brakes! That's almost your entire portfolio invested in a fairly risky asset.

Quickly see how your assets are allocated

And for our graphically minded folks, you'll most often see an asset allocation pie chart that visually represents what you own.

Here's a fun little ditty. You'll often hear the phrase "asset allocation" as a noun. In other words, this is my asset allocation. This means, here is how my portfolio is invested.

But you'll also hear "asset allocation" as a verb, as in the process of allocating or dividing up your investments into different asset classes.

The takeaway is that asset allocation simply looks at your portfolio of investments and tells you what asset classes you own and what the percentage of each is in your overall portfolio. Asset allocation is a thing – here is my asset allocation – but it's also a process.

The big question you may have is, "That's all nice and good. Now I know what asset allocation is, but *why* should my investments be allocated?" And that, my friends, is a very good question. The answer may surprise you. In the next lesson, I make the case that asset allocation is for losers.

ASSET ALLOCATION
IS FOR LOSERS

This lesson will get me in trouble...

Asset allocation is for losers?

We've spent several lessons on asset classes and asset allocation, but I'm going to let you in on a dirty little secret in the financial world that no one likes to admit to or talk about. Asset allocation, the process of choosing which asset classes and the amount to invest in, is for losers.

Yeah, you heard me right. Losers. Flunkies. Duds. Failures. Imbeciles. Morons.

Blasphemy! Asset allocation is sacred to investors and financial folks. How dare I discredit, desecrate, and defile this investment commandment?

What could possess me to do this? Well, the truth.

Forget about investing for a second. Imagine you and your friends just arrived in Vegas. You have $500 to gamble for the weekend. You sit down at a roulette wheel (wait, do you sit at a roulette wheel? I don't know. I guess you can tell how much I gamble!).

You put a little money on red, a little on 6, 18, 24, and 36. The ball spins, lands, and stops. You win or you lose. Whatever. That's not really the point. You spread your money around the table. Why? Well, it would be pretty crazy for you to put all your money on say, 22. Chances are low (and for you statisticians out there, it would be a 1 in 38 chance) that the ball would land on 22. If it landed on any of the other 37 numbers, you'd lose it all. You'd be done for the weekend.

Asset allocation is like spreading your money around the roulette table

So, of course, you don't do that. You spread your chips around the table so you don't lose it all at once.

But what if I was with you at this roulette table, and I had a secret formula that could predict, with 100% accuracy, what number the ball was going to land on every single time? Well, that would change everything, wouldn't it?

Would you put your money on 6, 18, 24, and 36? Would you spread your chips around the table? No way! You'd put all your chips on the number I told you would win. Yes, every single last chip you had, you'd put on just one number because you knew it would win. If I told you 13 was going to win, would you put some on 13, but also some on 18, 27, and 31? Of course not! You'd put it all on 13.

Okay, now back to investing. Why do we split our money up into different asset classes? Because we can't predict the future. We don't know which asset class is going to "win" or do the best. We don't know if U.S. large cap stocks will produce the best return next year or if emerging market bonds will do better. So what do we do? We put some here and some over there and even more there.

But if we could predict what asset class would do the best with 100% certainty, our asset allocation would look like this:

Your asset allocation if you could see into the future

So even though asset allocation is for losers, meaning some of what we invest in will not be the best performing asset class, it is still one of the most important things you can do as an investor to protect and build wealth.

In the next chapter I'll tell you a true story that almost ended in a disaster...

WHAT CAN HAPPEN IF YOU DON'T UNDERSTAND ASSET ALLOCATION

Scary true story…

I'm invested in what???

This is a true story. A new client came to me because she wanted to do some retirement planning. She already had an investment advisor, but she wanted me to review her portfolio. In less than 30 seconds, I determined several things that you can now determine as well. First, I looked at her main asset classes. How much did she have in stocks, bonds, cash, and real estate? Turns out, she was 98% in stocks. Okay, that tells you something. Then, I looked at the sub-asset class within stocks – looking at how much was in U.S. stocks, developed stocks, and emerging market stocks. Turns out, she had about 20% in U.S. stocks and 80% in emerging market stocks. Okay, that tells you something more. Then I looked at if she's invested in large or small companies. Turns out, she had about 50% of her portfolio in small stocks. Then I looked at what industries she was invested in. Turns out, she had about 60% of her portfolio in technology stocks.

Based on what you know, do you think someone retiring who needs some income and stability should have 98% in stocks? How about half of her portfolio in small stocks in emerging markets and the majority in just one industry?

She was shocked. She didn't realize what she owned or the risk she was taking. But if she had been money smart, she easily could have seen this for herself.

Even if you don't want to make the investment decisions yourself, the information you are learning here will help you understand much more and will help you work better with your advisors.

45

THE EPIC BATTLE BETWEEN RISK AND RETURN

Which side are you on?

How are risk & reward connected when it comes to investing?

What's a professional investment manager and a huge meathead at the gym have in common?

No pain, no gain! The buffed out beefcake wears this message on his muscle shirt, and the investment guy has this message in his brochure.

No pain, no gain! In essence, if you want to do well, there is going to be some pain involved. As an investor, the gain is, of course, making money, and the pain is losing money.

Here's how it plays out, at least in theory. The more investment risk you take, the more money you can make. In other words, if you are willing to invest in things that are quite volatile and could lose money, those same investments are the ones that could probably go up in value the most.

The higher the risk, the greater (usually) the reward

On the other hand, those investments that are more stable and have less risk of crashing probably won't shoot up in value overnight.

Generally speaking, risk and reward are connected when it comes to investing. Small cap stocks are more volatile and have a greater chance of losing money, but historically, they also have made a better return than larger company stocks.

Or take high yield bonds. Do you remember these? These are bonds that pay out a high interest rate, also called yield. Why do they pay a high interest rate? It's like lending money to a friend who is broke and out of work. There is a much greater chance you won't get your money back.

The big lesson here is when you see that such and such investment is projected to produce a 15% return when everything else is projected to produce an 8% return, you have to ask yourself, "How?" Higher return, so they must be taking more risk.

I'm not saying the investment is good or bad, but start thinking in terms of how higher return means you are taking more risk. If you do invest in this investment, would you want half of your money in it or maybe a smaller amount knowing that this is much riskier? Yeah, you'd probably want a smaller amount.

In the next lesson, I'm taking the gloves off. If you really want to get rich, stick with me. I'm going to show you how to become a millionaire almost instantly. Are you ready?

46

HOW TO BECOME A MILLIONAIRE BY TIMING THE MARKET

You don't want to miss this lesson!

Would you like to become a millionaire? Well, then this is the chapter for you. I'm going to show you how you can time the market to quickly and easily become a millionaire.

First things first. What does it mean to time the market? Okay, take out a stopwatch and – no, that would be silly. Not that kind of timing. When we say time the market, what we are really saying is move in and out of investments so you can buy when prices are low and sell when prices are high. Instead of taking a patient, long-term approach to investing, you want to quickly make gut reactions based on global economic and geopolitical events with the expectation that you will know the specific time to both buy an investment and also sell the investment.

Okay, so here's how you can become a millionaire with market timing. Start with a billion dollars and then try to time the market for a few months, and you'll almost certainly be worth a million by the end of it.

$1,000,000,000

– Time The Market

_____

$1,000,000

More money is lost on timing the market than gained

What? Was that sarcasm? Yes, my friends. That was sarcasm.

Timing the market is for chumps. Losers. Billionaires who lost nearly everything and now are millionaires.

But how can it be? It seems so reasonable. Doesn't it make sense to get in and then out at the right times?

Well, sure. If you could actually do it successfully, then it would make sense.

It's like being asked, "How can you win an Olympic Gold Medal?" That's easy. Just run the 100 meters in about 9 seconds.

Yeah, no kidding. But it's easier said than done.

Same is true for timing the market.

Don't get conned into the false belief that there is some investing guru who has a secret formula or algorithm for market timing. More money is lost on timing the market than gained.

Here are a few quotes on the matter from highly respected investors:

"A decade of results throws cold water on the notion that strategists exhibit any special ability to time the markets." — *The Wall Street Journal*

"Far more money has been lost by investors preparing for corrections, or trying to anticipate corrections, than has been lost in corrections themselves." — Peter Lynch

"Become a millionaire by first starting with a billion dollars and then trying to time the market." – Robert Pagliarini

And while this next guy is no Robert Pagliarini, he's got a pretty good track record.

"The only value of stock forecasters is to make fortunetellers look good." — Warren E. Buffett

The saying is, "It's not about timing the market, but time in the market." That makes all the difference.

But since you can't make money consistently from timing the market, is all lost? Should we forget about this whole investing thing altogether?

47

WHY YOU DON'T NEED TO TIME THE MARKET

You'll feel better about investing after this lesson

Okay, so you were so moved by the last chapter that you are sure you will not be successful timing the market and you're sure there isn't some investment expert or formula that can time the market either. Does this mean you are doomed as an investor?

Let's look at some real world data. This little bit was written for Charles Schwab, and I want to share it with you.

Imagine for a moment that you've just received a year-end bonus or income tax refund. You're not sure whether to invest now or wait. After all, the market recently hit an all-time high. Now imagine that you face this kind of decision every year — sometimes in up markets, other times in downturns. Is there a good rule of thumb to follow?

Because timing the market perfectly is, well, about as likely as winning the lottery, the best strategy for most of us mere mortal investors is not to try to market-time at all.

But don't take my word for it. Consider Schwab's research on the performance of five hypothetical long-term investors following very different investment strategies. Each received $2,000 at the beginning of every year for 20 years, ending in 2012, and left the money in the market. Check out how they did:

Peter Perfect was a perfect market timer. He had incredible skill (or luck) and was able to place his $2,000 into the market every year at the lowest monthly close. He continued to time his investments perfectly every year through 2012.

Ashley Action took a simple, consistent approach: Each year, once she received her cash, she invested her $2,000 in the market at the earliest possible moment.

Matthew Monthly divided his annual $2,000 allotment into 12 equal portions, which he invested at the beginning of each month.

Rosie Rotten had incredibly poor timing, or perhaps terribly bad luck. She invested her $2,000 each year at the market's peak.

Larry Linger left his money in cash investments (using Treasury bills as a proxy) every year and never got around to investing in stocks at all. He was always convinced that lower stock prices, and, therefore, better opportunities to invest his money, were just around the corner.

Here are the winners:

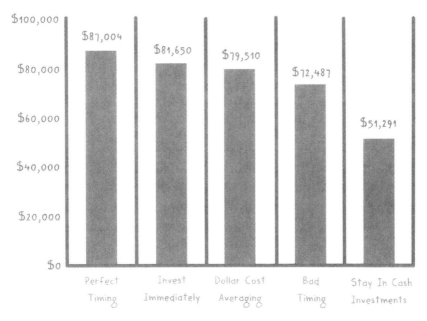

It's not about timing the market; it's time in the market.

What do you notice? Well, the perfect market timer, the investor who bought precisely at the very best times over the last 20 years, did the best. But look at the others. Other than the guy who didn't invest at all, they all did well. The takeaway is that you do not need to be extraordinary. You don't need a crystal ball to get a good investment return. Remember, it's not about timing the market; it's time in the market.

If that's the case, then why do so many people do so poorly? You'll find out what they do so wrong in the next lesson.

48

WHY ARE INVESTORS SO BAD AT INVESTING?

If cavemen were investors…

Have you heard of the caveman who was analytical, measured in his approach, and focused on long-term goals rather than short-term dangers? No? Yeah, me neither. That dude didn't live to be 12 years old. He's not a caveman, he's a cave boy.

All those wonderful personality characteristics would serve that cave boy today as a CEO or professional investor, but back then, in the face of constant dangers and threats, his highly emotional and act first and then ask questions later buddies survived through dinner.

And unfortunately for us today, these qualities of patience, analytical thinking, and long-term focus have only been developed recently in our evolution.

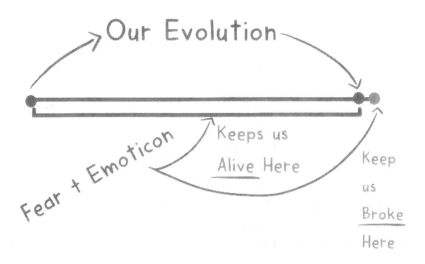

Too much fear & emotion will leave you broke

Investing takes certain qualities, such as taking a measured and analytical view rather than an emotional one and focusing on long-term goals that may be years or even decades in the future as opposed to what's happening right now.

For all you Trekkies, we are much more like the highly charged Dr. McCoy than we are Dr. Spock.

Let's have a look at these returns.

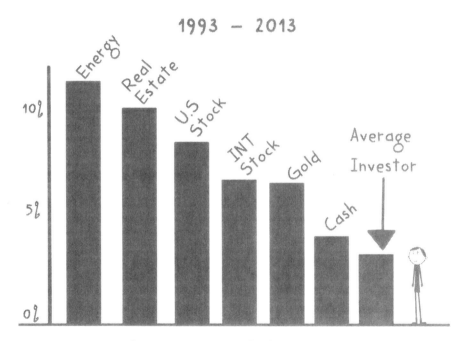

Why are investors so bad at investing?

Investors did terribly. It's as if someone took a $1 bill, $2 bill, $5 bill, $10 bill, $20 bill, and a $100 bill and put them all in a bag, shook it up, and then said, "Reach in, and grab yourself one bill." The average investor would reach in and pull out 50 cents.

Why do they do so badly, and more importantly, how can you do better?

1. **Know your risk tolerance.** This will help ensure that you don't have a portfolio that is too risky for your stomach.

2. **Stay grounded.** This means don't celebrate the gains and keep a long-term view on investing.

3. **Don't market time.** Trying to get out of the market and then back in at all the right times is impossible. And what's our lesson? How to become a millionaire? Start with a billion dollars and then try to time the market.

4. **Don't believe the hype.** Monitor your investments, but don't obsess over them. You have the ability to track your portfolio's every move minute by minute, but that won't keep you grounded. Check in each month and quarter, but don't get too crazy over watching everything all the time.

I'm trying to keep this G-rated, but I have to talk to you about pornography in the next lesson, and it's not going to be pretty.

THE DANGERS
OF FINANCIAL PORNOGRAPHY

The surefire way to lose all your money and get sent to the funny farm

Have you heard the breaking news story about the dog that bit a man? Of course not. That's not news. A dog biting someone is fairly routine. What about the news story about the man biting a dog? Maybe that was newsworthy about 20 years ago, but even that is blasé. To make news now, the man would have to bite a dog while riding a unicorn through a cotton candy rainbow.

Now that's news! Everything else is lame.

In the publishing world, the age old adage is, "If it bleeds, it leads." Magazines, newspapers, TV producers, and radio hosts have one and only one goal. It's not to inform; it's to hold your attention. That means they must titillate, frighten, and shock you with one story after another.

This is why the short pitches promoting that night's news are always, "There is a common household product in your kitchen slowly killing you and your family. News at 11." That will grab your attention and get you to tune into the 11 o'clock news broadcast.

We are programmed to respond to threats and fear. Remember poor cave boy? He was too cerebral and got eaten by a lion. Our ancestors, the ones who survived and reproduced, passed on the "oh crap" gene. Anything remotely scary or threatening grabs our attention. We then feel compelled to react.

The media are experts at exploiting this natural trait in each of us. What does this have to do with investing? A better question is what does this have to with bad investing? Everything.

Tune it all out

What makes most bad investors bad investors is not so much that they choose poor investments; often, the investments they chose are just fine. What makes them bad investors is they buy or sell at the wrong time. They hear a news story or read an article and it freaks them out so they sell. Then the market goes up and they get back in. Or they hear about a great fund that has done really well the past year and jump in, and then the fund doesn't do as well. They are constantly reacting to real or perceived threats and trading their investments – selling if they think the market is going to go down. Unfortunately, this is the one thing that almost guarantees they'll lose money – always getting out and then back into the market. It doesn't work.

Just today, I went to one of the most popular financial websites in the world and these three articles were front and center on the homepage:

"You should care about this warning of a sharp collapse."

"What to do when the S&P 500 nears its Zone of Death."

"This stock market is losing its cool. Here's what to do next."

Seriously. I didn't cherry-pick the website or the timing. I went to the website and just looked at the top of the homepage, and these were the headlines. And it's always like this. It's always, "the world is ending, so get out," or, "things are going to skyrocket, so you'd better get in." And the really disturbing thing is these sell now/buy now headlines can occur on the same day! You'll often see them on the homepage at the same exact time.

And just for the fun of it, I went onto the website a couple of days later and here were the headlines:

"The signs that say a stock market correction is close."

"Traders take cover for fear of big shift in market mood."

"Not-so-secret ingredient: Ikea's Swedish meatballs."

It would be comical if it didn't cost investors so much money.

The takeaway? If you follow the markets too closely, watch the business TV networks, read too many financial blogs, or listen to too many financial experts, you'll be inclined to want to "do something." That something is often to buy or sell, and it is usually the worst thing you can do. All this financial chatter, or as it is often called, "financial pornography," is just a bunch of media people trying to get you to click or tune in. They are not trying to educate you. They are not trying to help you become better investors. They are trying to scare the you-know-what out of you so you keep coming back day after day to figure out what you should do next. Stop sucking on the financial fear teat. Grow up and see the world and the games they are playing for what they really are. One of the best decisions you can make as an investor is to turn the noise off. If you did just that one thing, you'd dramatically boost your investment performance, and as a side benefit, sleep a little better at night.

Okay, the next lesson is the one you've been waiting for. I reveal the one investment trick you need to know. This is one you won't want to miss.

50

THE ONE INVESTMENT TRICK YOU NEED TO KNOW

If you only read one chapter, this is the one...

For the next ten seconds, stop everything you're doing.

You just learned the investment trick. In case you missed it, let's try it again. Imagine you just heard that a well-known financial guru has predicted the market is going to crash in the coming weeks. Here is the investment trick: stop everything you're doing.

Did you catch it?

You paused. You didn't react. You didn't text your advisor. You paused.

That's one of the best things you can do as an investor. Do nothing. Pause. Reflect. Think. Examine. Channel your inner cave boy. Don't just do something. Sit there.

51

DON'T BELIEVE THE HYPE: KNOWING WHAT'S POSSIBLE VS. WHAT'S PROBABLE

Knowing the difference could make or break your investment success

Which of the following is possible?

☐ North Korean cyber-terrorists can hack into our banking system and wipe out our wealth.

☐ A magnitude 15 earthquake strikes in California causing the state to sink into the Pacific Ocean.

☐ Artificially intelligent robots replace 99% of global jobs leaving the population without work and income.

☐ The U.S. government could eliminate the Federal Reserve and go back to a gold standard.

☐ A large scale electromagnetic pulse could be detonated over the United States destroying our power grid, cells phone networks, TVs, radios, and the electronics in our vehicles.

If you answered yes to all of these, you get a gold star! All of these doomsday threats are possible. It's hard to argue that any of the above threats (or any others you've heard) could never happen. They absolutely could happen. Every single one of them. In fact, it's possible all five of them could happen on the same day!

However, now ask yourself which of them are *probable*.

As an investor, the difference between possible and probable is one of the most important lessons you can learn. Why? Early on as an advisor, I'd have clients frantically call me because they read something or saw a video about some impending disaster. Their immediate response was fear that they'd be hurt or that the stock market would crash and wipe out their wealth. As a novice, I'd get a bit frantic myself. However, once I got past the scary headline and did more research, I'd find that the chance of the threat was ridiculously small.

Could an asteroid strike Manhattan killing millions and decimating the country's economy and financial system? Yes! But is it probable? Not at all.

Once you've asked yourself if the threat is probable, you can then ask yourself if the threat is actionable. Is there anything you can do to protect yourself or your wealth? If you're watching late night TV or listening to the radio, the solution might be "Buy gold!" The thinking is that gold will always have some value and that if the country or the financial system collapsed you could use gold. It's a bit of a longshot, but let's just say that was true. Okay, so you sell all of your investments and you buy gold. For how long? Forever? Until the asteroid hits? And this is where things start to *not* make a lot of sense.

You are afraid that a one in a bazillion (yes, that's a highly sophisticated financial figure) event will occur and you'll lose your money so you sell everything (incurring taxable gains) and buy gold which is highly volatile and regularly drops in value by double digits? This, my dear reader, is what they mean by jumping out of the pan and into the fire.

Wasn't it Newton who said every action has an equal and opposite reaction? The same is true here. Before you give in to a fear-based headline or scary YouTube video prophesizing the collapse of something or the other, ask yourself what the consequences of your reaction might be. Every single time I've done this with a client, the reaction posed a much greater threat to their wealth than the fear they were trying to avoid.

In the aftermath of the financial crisis, I visited a potential client at her house. She had several million dollars but was worried that another financial crisis would occur and wipe out the world's entire financial system. She didn't want to invest or do any traditional financial planning. Instead, she was building a shelter and learning how to create a sustainable garden in her backyard. The threat was possible, but it was not probable. If her worst-case need-to-live-off-the-land doomsday scenario came true, her money in the bank would probably be worthless anyway. Sadly for her, she missed out on over $3 million of investment gains because she was so focused on what was possible that she didn't want to consider if it was probable or the consequences of her reaction.

Before you make an emotional move, first ask yourself if the threat is possible (it always is) and then ask yourself if the threat is probable. Doing this will help you stay calm and will help you keep your wealth.

ACCOUNT OWNERSHIP? WHAT'S THAT?

It's not as simple as you think…

I'm all for starting slowly. Get started with something comfortably, and then gradually make things a bit more difficult.

Unfortunately, brokerage firms, RIAs, and discount brokerages don't take this same approach.

Let's say you get up the courage to start investing. You've gone through this book, and you feel you are money smart. You are excited about putting your money to work. You navigate to Charles Schwab or Fidelity and download a new account application. You've made it! Your troubles are behind you. It's nothing but sunshine and smiles from here.

And then you get to question number one on the application. WTF?! Before they even ask for your name or phone number, they hit you with some question about account ownership. They give you a bunch of options and tell you in big bold black letters, "Please check only one box."

It's like going to See's Candies and being told, "Just choose one." That's too much pressure! Do you get the fudge or the caramel?! I don't know!

Why do they have to make it so confusing?!

And although I'm in no way trying to undermine the significance of chocolate, the investment application and your financial future are both pretty important as well.

Here are the options you will most likely see: Individual, Joint Tenants with Right of Survivorship, Tenants in Common, Community Property, Community Property with Right of Survivorship, and Tenants by the Entirety.

If you thought choosing between the dark almond or the butterscotch square was tough, then this is absurd.

But what do all of these choices mean? Tenants by the Entirety? Really?

I'm really hesitating to go through each of these. There's no way you're going to remember, and frankly, why would you? I'd guess that 95% of advisors couldn't accurately tell you what each of these mean. Seriously.

I think the better lesson is to understand generally what this question about account ownership is all about. Because it's actually very, very, very important.

Account ownership is kind of what it sounds like. It is who owns this account. I'd say that is fairly important.

Since we're on a dessert kick with this lesson, let's continue it.

Imagine you love ice cream. Yes, hard to imagine. I know.

If you lived alone, all the ice cream cartons in your freezer would be yours. Nobody else's. Just yours. Well, that's an individual account. All the money, assets, and decisions are yours and yours alone.

But let's say you lived with your girlfriend or your spouse. Now, all that delicious ice cream may not be yours entirely. You may have to share it. That's what the other account ownership types are all about.

Not only do the different account ownership types affect who has access to the money and who owns it while you are alive, but they also say what happens if you pass away. Does your ice cream automatically go to your girlfriend, or does it instead go to your brother who lives down the street?

Selecting the correct account ownership is super important. It's good to know what this means, but definitely get some help in checking the right bubble.

But is there another way to build and protect wealth? This next lesson is huge. It can make or break how you do as an investor. Seriously.

WHAT IS RISK TOLERANCE?

Get me out!

Investing. You buy some stocks and mutual funds and watch your money grow like this over time.

Fantasy

Wouldn't this be nice?

This is not what happens though. This is more like what happens.

Reality

Unfortunately, investing is more of a roller coaster

What does this represent? This shows the value of your portfolio, or maybe just a stock or mutual fund. Basically, it shows how the prices of your investments change all the time. When the stock market is open, you can see how your investments are doing in real time. Up, down, up, up, down, up. Prices move. This is called volatility. An investment with no volatility means the price never changes. It's always the same. An investment with high volatility means the investment experiences big price changes day-to-day, week-to-week, and month-to-month.

So let's talk about these ups and downs. What if you had money invested and you woke up and saw on the news that the stock market was down 10% that day? And then you looked at your portfolio and saw you were down big, too? What would you be thinking? What would you be feeling? This gets to the heart of our comfort level with big swings in the value of our portfolio and investments. Of course, no one minds big moves up. That is universally accepted as a good thing! No, we're talking about the big drops. When you go online and see losses, maybe big losses in a day or maybe when you are reviewing your monthly statement. "I lost how much?!" That, my friend, is volatility.

As an investor, that is something we must live with. Unless you leave your money in cash or buy CDs from your bank, investments can go up and down. Of course, over time, we anticipate they will go up in value, otherwise we would never buy them to begin with, but they can, and will, go down in value, too.

How much does it bother you to see losses? On a scale of 1 to 10, where 1 is, "I can't sleep and all I can think about is how much money I've lost," and 10 is, "Whatever. Investments go up, they go down. It's all part of investing," what number are you?

How much risk are you comfortable taking?

What we're talking about is risk tolerance. How much risk or volatility can you tolerate before you freak out? How much up and down can you handle without it being a big deal?

Some people see the market drop 10% and they start thinking about living under a bridge and eating from a garbage can, whereas other people see the market drop 10% and start thinking, "This is great because now I can buy some investments on sale!" Same event, two completely different reactions.

There are questionnaires and online tools available that aim to help you determine your risk tolerance. "But why? Who cares?" you might ask.

Well, it turns out knowing your risk tolerance is actually pretty important, and it can actually make you a better investor and help you make more money.

Intrigued now? Maybe I should have opened this chapter with that line. Anyway, in the next lesson, I'll show you how it works.

54

HOW TO MAKE MORE MONEY BY KNOWING YOUR RISK TOLERANCE

Lessons from Clueless Karen and Insightful Irene

You are now an expert on risk tolerance! Congratulations. But who cares? As the familiar saying goes, "You can't pay your rent with risk tolerance."

Well, now, maybe you can.

Let's look at an example of two people: Clueless Karen and Insightful Irene.

Clueless Karen has never heard of risk tolerance and is definitely not money smart. She just started investing because she thought it was the right thing to do.

Insightful Irene, on the other hand, has read a brilliant financial self-help book and understands volatility and her own risk tolerance. What happens as each of them invests?

Stop and breathe – don't act emotionally and irrationally!

Imagine they both wake up on the same day, and they notice the market is down 5%. Clueless Karen wasn't prepared for this. Her investments were quite risky and her portfolio is down 10%. She can't handle the loss. She immediately decides to sell everything because she just can't bear to see any more losses.

Insightful Irene looks at her portfolio. She sees that it is down 2%.

She's not happy, but 2% is not a disaster. She goes about her day, not thinking about it again.

What's happened here? Clueless Karen acted emotionally and irrationally. She wasn't thinking about the long-term value of her investments or her overall financial plan. She made her entire decision based on how she was feeling about the losses. And guess what? This is how humans make decisions. We do not have a logical Dr. Spock-like response. We feel and we react, not to facts, but to emotions. The problem with this approach is that our emotions can cause us to act in ways that may not be in our long-term best interest.

Insightful Irene is just as scared of risk and volatility as Clueless Karen. She hates losses and is just as emotional and prone to making bad decisions. But—and this is why she's insightful—she understands this about herself. She knows she would react just as emotionally as Karen if her portfolio was down 10%. This is why she invested her money differently. More safely. With less volatile investments. This way, she loses less and won't have the same gut wrenching feeling and won't make quick emotional trades.

The power isn't so much knowing your risk tolerance, but knowing your risk tolerance and allowing that to guide how you invest. You want your portfolio invested in a way that is closely aligned with your ability to withstand volatility and short-term losses.

If Clueless Karen had known her risk tolerance, she never would have been so aggressively invested, and she wouldn't have lost 10% that day, and she wouldn't have sold everything, and she wouldn't have kicked herself when the market went up 25% the next year.

Be like Insightful Irene. Know your risk tolerance. It will make you a better long-term investor.

But that's just part of the story. A lot of people are quite nervous about investing and worried about seeing their investments go up and down. Let's dig into that a bit more next.

55

WHAT IS THE BEST WAY TO HANDLE THE UPS AND DOWNS IN THE MARKET?

How to avoid the #1 mistake investors make…

This is kind of a trick question. How will you possibly handle the ups in the market? Those stressful days, weeks, and months where you look at your accounts and they just keep going up, and all you can think of is all the money you are making? How will you handle this? Therapy?

Of course, it's not the ups that are really the problem. It's the downs that can cause anxiety, sleepless nights, and fear.

But, I think you'll be a better investor if you approach both the ups and the downs similarly. It's about approaching the market and investing with a healthy perspective.

The investors who celebrate the ups and the highs are the same ones who suffer the most when the market is down.

It's like that friend you have who is nuts about your local sports team. They go crazy when they are winning – they are on top of the world and nothing could be better. And then they go nearly comatose and depressed when their team is losing. And there are some people, you know who you are, who experience these high highs and low lows not just during the season, but during each game!

As an investor, this is a terrible existence. It will give you an ulcer, and it will drive you to drink. This kind of emotional involvement is not sustainable. You will crack, and that's not pretty. What does cracking look like? Well, I suppose it could include lithium and white coats, but here's what cracking normally looks like.

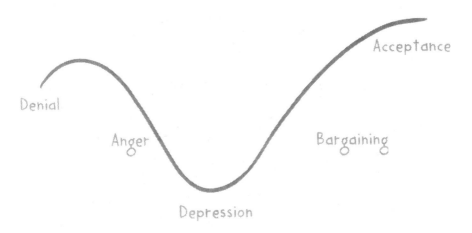

The stages of grief, investment edition

Think back to March of 2009. Our country was in the middle of a nasty recession. Markets plunged nearly 50% from their peaks. Unemployment was high. The banking and financial industries nearly collapsed. We were on the precipice. But we also had a government that was throwing nearly a trillion dollars at the problem. We still had companies who were selling goods. We still had people who were working. Things were bad, but it wasn't the end times. Investors were discouraged, to say the least. They saw their portfolios drop by 25% or more.

Instead of telling you what cracking looks like, how about I tell you what it sounds like? "Get me out." That's the call many advisors received. Cracking is deciding that you just can't stomach any more losses, despite having a reasonable allocation and long-term investment horizon, and selling everything and going to cash. *Stop the bleeding* is the phrase that comes to mind.

But it's unfortunate. As an investor, you don't invest for a quick buck. You invest for years and you have to go in thinking that there will be losses at some point. Let me repeat that. I tell my clients over and over again, you will lose money! That's not a commercial slogan or tagline you'll often see: "Invest with us. We guarantee you'll lose money." But it's true. As an investor, there will be periods of time when your account will go down.

It's important to recognize this and to prepare mentally for it. This way, when it happens, and it will, it doesn't take you by surprise.

But what's the problem with just selling and going to cash once in a while after the market drops? You can't effectively sell and then buy at the right times. Remember, this is called market timing, and it's how to become a millionaire – you start with a billion and then market time, and you'll likely end up with a million. It just doesn't work.

The clients who said, "Get me out!" in March 2009 got out at the low. From early March until now, the market has gone up 100%.

The takeaway? Know your risk tolerance and put together a portfolio that matches the amount of risk you want to take. Expect that you will lose money. Really anticipate that it will happen. Imagine checking your portfolio online and seeing nothing but red. It will happen. Inoculate yourself. Lastly, don't celebrate the ups and the highs. Take a more measured approach. The best approach is to think and truly believe that the market goes up and the market goes down. Over time, I expect that the value of my account will go up, but in the short-term, anything can and will happen.

WHAT'S THIS GONNA COST?

The four letter f word that's worse than the other four letter f word

| F | | | | ! |

This can't end well...

Let's play "complete the word." We know it's a bad word. We know it starts with "f." We know it has four letters. We know this book is rated PG-13. So that must mean the word is F E E S.

Yup, fees. Those nasty buggers that strip away your hard-earned money. The bad news is they are inevitable, but the good news is you will learn the many forms they take and how to reduce them.

Let's get started.

Transaction fees. Transaction fees are usually flat fees for buying or selling an investment. They tend to not be that much. They could be $10 to $50, typically. For example, if you want to buy 1, 100, or 10,000 shares of Disney, you'd have this flat fee.

Commissions. Those are the fees you pay your broker or advisor. They are usually a certain percent of the total transaction. The bigger your buy or sell order, the bigger the commission. Think about selling your house. If you sell for $100,000, the standard 5% commission is $5,000. If you sell for $200,000, the same standard 5% commission is now $10,000.

Loads. Okay, so how to explain these? They suck. I don't even need to tell you what they are. All you need to know is they suck. If something sucks, it's probably a wise idea to avoid it. Pop quiz. Should you buy an investment with a load? NO!

Fine, I'll tell you what loads are. A load is like a commission. If you want to buy an investment with a load, you have to pay a certain percentage for the right and the privilege to invest in the investment.

How sweet and kind of them! For example, if the load is 5% and you invest $100,000, only $95,000 is going into the investment and the other $5,000 is going into someone's pocket. How not so sweet and kind of them.

But that's not all! If you order now, you'll get screwed even further. Investors noticed these loads and they didn't seem to like them, so instead of getting rid of the loads (that would be silly), the investment folks said, "No problem. We understand. You don't have to pay us any load when you buy the investment. Aren't we nice? Oh, but by the way, when you sell the fund, there's going to be a load." If this program wasn't PG, I'd say a series of F words right about now.

I better stop right here for this chapter. I'm getting too worked up. But don't worry: I'll be back in the next lesson to talk to you about something very important when it comes to investing. You won't want to miss it.

WHAT'S AN EXPENSE RATIO?

Oh, joy! More fees!

Well, isn't this your lucky day! We get to talk about how to triple your money in less than a month with a no-risk secret strategy. What's that? It doesn't exist? So, now what? Well, it looks like I won't be sharing that secret, but I have something just as exciting. I'm going to talk to you more about fees!

This next one is actually common and important. You'll want to know about it.

The first is an expense ratio. When you invest in an individual stock or bond, you pay the transaction fee or maybe a commission, but then that's it. There is no ongoing "management." You own the stock and that's that. But, when you buy a mutual fund or ETF, for example, the idea is that you are buying a basket of investments and that this basket of investments takes expertise to manage throughout the year. You have people, investment managers, who are buying and selling investments within the mutual fund or ETF. This is especially true for active managers, but even with a passive index fund, there are still some trades that occur and some expenses. That website where you can log in and see your portfolio or the statement that comes each month will cost you money.

$100,000 Investment

1% Expense Ratio

———————————————

$1,000 Annual Fee

It's easy enough to calculate and understand

Okay, so back to expense ratios. This is the fee you pay these managers. It is a flat percentage that represents an annual fee. For example, if the expense ratio is 1% and you have $100,000 invested, the annual fee would be $1,000. If you had $1 million invested, the annual fee would be $10,000.

As you can imagine, expense ratios vary widely. Some funds charge 2% or more per year, while others charge as little as 0.05%. That's a huge difference. Active managers almost always have a higher expense ratio than passive index managers. Sometimes, it depends on what the manager invests in. Think about this: if you were investing in large U.S. companies, there is a lot of information about companies such as Google, Coca Cola, Wal-Mart, and others. But if your mutual fund invests in small technology companies in sub-Saharan Africa, it might cost you a lot more to do research on these companies and to have analysts on the ground talking to the owners. There may even be currency exchange rate fees and government fees. It could very well cost the fund more in fees just to invest in these kinds of companies.

So, unless you plan on only investing in individual stocks and bonds, you will probably pay fees in the form of expense ratios on your funds. How much you pay depends on many factors, but the biggest factor is your decision to invest in active or passive index funds.

Do you have a sense of an expense ratio? You can easily find the expense ratio of any mutual fund or ETF online. In fact, that's your homework. Go to Yahoo! Finance and type in the mutual fund symbol for VFIAX. It's the Vanguard S&P 500 Index Fund. Then click on "Profile" and you'll see a section titled "Fees & Expenses." Check it out.

What else can you check out? Me in the next lesson. I'm going to discuss AUM. What's AUM? You'll get your Ph.D. in AUM ASAP.

58

WHAT ARE ASSET UNDER MANAGEMENT FEES?

Sounds complicated but it's not…

Make sure you understand all the fees you're paying, and total them up

You've learned about all kinds of fees and expenses you may pay as an investor, but there's still one more. And this is a popular one. These are Assets Under Management fees (also called "AUM").

Again, this last type of fee is also pretty common. Financial planners and investment advisors may help you determine your risk tolerance, come up with an appropriate asset allocation based on your age and other factors, help you choose the investments for your portfolio initially, and monitor those investments over time – buying and selling as needed. There will be a fee for this service. That's where the investment advisory fee comes in. It is often a percentage fee of the assets they manage for you. This is the asset under management fee. If they charge 1% and they manage $100,000 for you, you will pay them $1,000 a year. If you have $1 million they manage for you, they will charge $10,000 per year.

So, as you can see, there can be more than one layer of fees. You may pay an investment advisor 1% a year to manage your money, and that investment advisor may suggest you purchase a mutual fund that has an expense ratio of 0.50%. In that case, you'd be paying 1% to your advisor and half a percent to the mutual fund manager for a total of 1.50%.

When you are looking at fees, make sure you look at all the fees you are paying. Total them all up to see what you're really paying.

As a rule of thumb, it's best if your investment advisory fee is 1% or less and the total of your other fees is less than 1%, too. You should have no problem having your total expenses per year be 2% or less. If either fee or both combined are more than 2%, you should dig deeper. Find out why.

59

WHAT YOU NEED TO KNOW ABOUT RETIREMENT ACCOUNTS

You'll be (nearly) an expert when you're done!

Do you know what would be really cool? If we had just one kind of retirement account with simple rules for putting money in and taking it out. Keep dreaming! We don't. We have so many different kinds of retirement accounts – all with crazy ridiculous rules, half of which you wouldn't even believe if I told you. It's almost as if the geniuses who designed all of these accounts actually didn't want us to save for retirement. Honestly, I don't think you could do anything to make them more complicated and less user-friendly.

So what do most people do in the face of mind-numbingly difficult rules and systems? They read the fine print and rationally weigh pros and cons of each account in a systematic manner aimed at maximizing options and eventual net value? Well, it's either that, or do nothing and hope for the best.

But not you! You are getting money smart! Here's the least you need to know about the most common retirement accounts. Here's what most of them have in common:

- **Retirement**. They are retirement accounts. This means their purpose is for, you guessed it, retirement. This is money you put away today for when you retire. So they are all really set up for the long-term. They make it hard for you to pull money out before you retire. You might get hit with penalties and other restrictions. Again, it's called a retirement account for a reason!

- **Invest**. You get to invest this money in mutual funds, stocks, bonds, or other types of investments, if you want. It's not designed to be a savings account that sits in cash. Since the money is for a far off retirement, you are encouraged to invest it.

- **Tax**. You get to save income tax now. The money you put into the retirement account reduces the amount of money you have to report to the IRS, which means because you have a lower income, you are taxed less. And here's the catch. Even though you benefit from paying less tax now, eventually, the IRS is going to want their tax. That's why these accounts are sometimes called "tax deferred." It means you're not paying tax on it now, but rather you are deferring it to the future when you take money out of your account. What's so great about that? Your account gets to grow over the years (and possibly decades) without you having to pay any tax.

Okay, so those are the things that are similar about most of the retirement accounts. Now let's break the retirement accounts into two main categories:

Company Plans

Company plans are those offered through an employer. In other words, you have to work for a company to be able to open and save in one of these accounts.

Company plans are only offered through an employer

401(k). This is the granddaddy of company-sponsored retirement plans. Many employers offer these to their employees. As an employee, you can take some of the income you'd normally get in your paycheck and have it deposited into your 401(k) account instead. So instead of getting $1,000 in your paycheck, you might decide to invest $100 in your 401(k) account, so you'd get $900 as your paycheck. There are a few cool things about 401(k)s. First, you're able to contribute quite a bit of money each year into it, more than many of the other retirement accounts. Second, some companies will even put some extra money in your 401(k) account for you! This is called a match, and it's free money to you.

Okay, there are a lot of other retirement accounts through companies such as SEP IRAs, Simple IRAs, defined benefit plans, profit sharing plans, and many, many more. They all have different rules. It's nuts, but that's how it is.

Individual Plans

Unlike the company plans that require an actual company, individual plans don't! Almost anyone can set these up on their own.

IRA. This is called an individual retirement account. You get to contribute money and it grows tax-deferred. You might even get a tax deduction. The main difference is you can't contribute as much into an IRA as you can with a 401(k).

Roth IRA. Okay, this one is a bit different from the others. Remember how I said you might be able to reduce your taxes with a 401(k) or IRA? Well, with a Roth IRA, forget about that. You can't save any taxes now, no matter how much you contribute. And at this point, you may be thinking, "Why would anyone want to put money in a Roth IRA?" Even though you don't get any kind of tax deduction when you put the money in, it grows tax free; and unlike the others, when you take money out of the Roth IRA, you don't have to pay tax! Do you see the difference? With most retirement accounts, you get a tax break when you put the money in, but then you have to pay tax when you take the money out. With a Roth, you pay the tax when you put it in but not when you take it out. Why does that matter? Well, it may make more sense for you to pay the tax now, or it may be better to pay the tax later. It depends on a lot of different options, but just know there are different accounts, depending on which strategy is better for you.

Annuities. I could do an entire video or course about annuities. There are so many different kinds and options that it would make your head spin, but let's touch on a couple of main ideas with annuities. An annuity is an investment where you contribute money and hope for a return. An annuity is different from other investments in that some annuities provide certain guarantees. For example, the annuity company, an insurance company, will guarantee a certain minimum rate of return. They might say, "You give us money and we'll give you a 5% return each year," kind of like a CD investment. They might also guarantee a certain amount of income for as long as you live, kind of like Social Security, so no matter how long you live you keep getting a check in the mail. Again, there are lots of different flavors of annuities, but the guarantees are what set annuities apart from most other investments.

That's your lesson on retirement accounts. Don't worry about all of the details. At this point, the lesson is simply that there are special accounts designed to help people save for retirement. The two main types are (1) those provided by a company and (2) those that an individual can do.

The most common company-provided retirement account is the 401(k) or 403(b), although there are dozens of others, each with their own rules. The most common individual retirement plans are regular IRAs, Roth IRAs, and annuities.

Most people don't just choose one, but instead, and most often, investors will have several different types. Again, don't get caught up in the rules for all of them; it's not important at this point. All you need to know to be money smart is that these special accounts exist and they can help you save for your retirement.

60

SO, HOW DID
MY INVESTMENT DO?

Why your 10% return is bad and why your -5% return is great

Should you be happy or sad?

If you finish a game of bowling, you can see your score. After you take the SAT, you see how you did. If you invest, you can see what return you got. Simple.

But it's not quite that simple.

If I told you I just shot an 85 but that I've never played a round of golf in my life, what would you think? If you know anything about golf, and I know very little, a score of 85 is considered good. You'd probably think I was a natural and some kind of golf prodigy. You might even call me the next Tiger Woods.

Speaking of Tiger, if he shot an 85, what would we think? Well, we don't have to imagine. He shot an 85 and it was nearly a CNN breaking news story. The media was all over this saying it was the "worst round of his PGA tour career."

In short, my 85 would be exalted, but his was ridiculed. Same score, completely different interpretations.

So let's bring this back to investing because this is a fair question, "How did I do?" The question, though, is not complete. How did you do? "Compared to what?" is the only legitimate answer.

The real question should be, "How did I do compared to other investments or portfolios like mine?" Now that is meaningful. How is an 85 in golf? Meaningless. How is an 85 in golf for a beginner? For a pro? Now that is meaningful.

So how can you compare how you did with others? This is where you can look at indexes. Remember, those are baskets of investments that track a particular asset class. For example, the S&P 500 index is one of the most popular indexes and it tracks how well large companies in the U.S. do. But there are also indexes for bonds, energy companies, small companies, international companies, etc. There is an index for everything, so you can compare your portfolio against an index.

And this is why you can be upset with a positive 10% return but thrilled with losing 5%. Back in 2008, the stock market did poorly. It was down over 30%. If you looked at the performance of your portfolio for 2008 and you were down 5%, you'd be thrilled. You'd throw yourself a party. You were down only 5%, but the overall stock market was down over 30%. That's pretty darn good.

But fast forward a couple of years to 2013. You're looking at your portfolio and you got a 10% return. You think about throwing yourself a party, but "compared to what" is lingering in your head, so you look at what the stock market did overall. Turns out, it was up just about 30%. Hmm. Suddenly you don't feel in a party mood.

"Compared to what?" is key. Always come back to "compared to what?"

If you see an ad for a mutual fund and they report, "Our fund was up 50% last year," what question are you going to ask? Okay, but compared to what? If they invested in small Indian biotech companies focused on cancer cures, then let's see how the index for small Indian companies focused on cancer cures did last year. Up 100%? Then this fund underperformed. Up 10%? Then this fund is awesome!

I'm being a bit facetious, but you get the point. Compared to what? Always come back to "compared to what?"

A discerning investing student may be thinking, "This makes sense, but if my portfolio is invested in stocks, bonds, energy, and other asset classes, does it really make sense to compare it to just how the stock market did?"

So, let me address it. If I ask you to compare a steak from Denny's to a steak from Morton's, that's not really a fair comparison. The Denny's steak should be compared to Carrows and Coco's. The Morton's steak should be compared to Ruth's Chris and Capital Grille. You have to compare apples to apples.

If you are a conservative investor with half your portfolio in bonds and the other half in stocks, it's not really fair to compare your performance with just stocks or with just bonds. You'd want to see how your stocks did against a stock index and how your bonds did against a bond index. This will give you a much better idea of how you did compared to similar investments.

Remember, always come back to "compared to what?" to really figure out how you did.

61

SHOULD I REINVEST DIVIDENDS?

And the answer is...

Remember when we talked about the two ways to make money as an investor? Come on! It wasn't that long ago, was it? The two ways are (1) the value of the investment goes up and (2) income. So if you buy a house for $100,000 and it goes up to $125,000, that $25,000 is growth, or appreciation. That's one way to make money. The second way is if the investment provides you with income. Take that house you bought for $100,000. Let's say it didn't go up at all and stayed stuck at $100,000. Could you still make money? You bet! If you had a renter paying you $2,000 a month, you'd make $24,000 a year in rental income.

So let's talk a bit more about that second way to make money – through income. Income from investments is like Lady Gaga – it can take many different forms. Income can be interest, dividends, rental income, or capital gain distributions. It's not so important to get hung up on what each of these is at this point. The lesson is that some investments pay income.

The question is what should you do with that income? If you had that rental property and were getting $2,000 a month, what could you do with it? Well, you could take it down to the local bingo game each month. You could have a killer party with all your friends each month. You could lease a beautiful Rolls Royce. What do all of these have in common? Besides being a lot of fun, they are all examples of you using the rental income. You're spending it.

What's another option for the $2,000 a month of income? Well, what if you were to take that money and invest in more rental properties? Hmm. Now that could be interesting.

And this is your choice as an investor. When you buy a mutual fund or stock, you are often given a choice: do you want to reinvest

FREE
MONEY SMART VIDEO SERIES

MONEYSMARTCOURSE.COM

dividends, interest, or capital gain distributions back into the investment, or do you want to just leave these distributions in cash?

When you reinvest the income back into the investment, you are taking advantage of compound investing. This is a powerful multiplier. This is like the martial art of Aikido, where you use your opponent's energy against them. In this case, you are using your investment's income to add more to your investment.

It can mean the difference of thousands of dollars to you, the investor.

Of course, if you are retired and need the cash to live on, that's one thing, but if you don't need the cash, you can use your investments to buy more investments.

The takeaway? I like reinvesting income and dividends. Unless you have a really good reason otherwise, say yes to reinvesting!

And if that wasn't convincing enough, in the next lesson, you'll learn why re-investing is so powerful and a popular quote from Einstein that Einstein never actually said. Oh, the suspense is killing me!

MAKING MONEY WITH COMPOUND INVESTING

This is the real "secret" to creating wealth

Have you heard this quote from Einstein? "Compound interest is the most powerful force in the universe." No? That's okay because he actually never said it. It's one of those quotes that financial folks like me repeat because it sounds good and makes us look smart.

That's okay, though. Just because Einstein didn't actually say it doesn't mean compound interest, or even better, compound investing, isn't incredibly powerful.

Let's learn what it is, and then I'll show you just how amazing it is.

It's been said making your first million is the hardest – I believe it was Einstein. What does this mean?

It means that accumulating the first million dollars is harder than getting your second or third or fourth. But why is this? In part, compound investing.

At its most basic, compound investing is this: I work for my money, and then my money works for me. But it gets even better. It's more than just having your money make money. It's having the money your money makes make more money. Say that five times fast!

Bam! Now that is what I'm talking about. This is the power of compound investing and how you can create massive wealth.

WHAT IS DOLLAR COST AVERAGING?

This is a great strategy for most people...

This is a phrase you might hear from time to time. Dollar cost averaging. It's kind of a cool technique, and you should be somewhat familiar with what it is, as it can help you make more money as an investor.

Let's look at two investors in terms of the fable *The Tortoise and the Hare.* Remember that one? The tortoise and the rabbit decide to race each other. The rabbit, obviously much faster, takes off and is in the lead. The tortoise, being a tortoise, is quite slow. He plods along in the race. Who wins? Spoiler alert. In a flash of literary surprise, the slow plodding turtle wins the race! Let's see how our investors do:

Purchase	Amount Invested		Price Per share		Number of Shares Purchased	
Date	Hare	Tortoise	Investor A	Investor B	Investor A	Investor B
Jan. 1	$5,000	$1,000	$10.00	$10.00	500	100
Feb. 1	$0	$1,000		$7.00	n/a	142
Mar. 1	$0	$1,000		$9.00	n/a	111
Apr. 1	$0	$1,000		$5.00	n/a	200
May 1	$0	$1,000		$12.00	n/a	83
	Total Invested		Average Price Per Share		Total Shares Purchased	
	$5,000	$5,000	$10.00	$8.60	500	636

With dollar cost averaging, you are taking the same dollar amount and investing it over time into a stock with the goal of buying into the stock at different prices. In this example, the tortoise wins! Yay! But honestly, I always hated that story. Would the hare really be so stupid to take a nap right before the finish line? So, let's look at another example of what could happen in the real world.

Purchase	Amount Invested		Price Per share		Number of Shares Purchased	
Date	Hare	Tortoise	Investor A	Investor B	Investor A	Investor B
Jan. 1	$5,000	$1,000	$10.00	$10.00	500	100
Feb. 1	$0	$1,000		$11.00	n/a	90
Mar. 1	$0	$1,000		$14.00	n/a	71
Apr. 1	$0	$1,000		$12.00	n/a	83
May 1	$0	$1,000		$15.00	n/a	67
	Total Invested		Average Price Per Share		Total Shares Purchased	
	$5,000	$5,000	$10.00	$12.40	500	411

And just like that, our sprightly bunny wins this race! Suck on that, shell boy.

So what is an investor to do? Sometimes you may not have a wad of cash to invest at once. For example, people who contribute to a 401(k) are really dollar cost averaging. With every paycheck throughout the year, they are taking part of their income and investing.

But sometimes you may have a lot of cash. For example, if you receive an inheritance or receive a lawsuit settlement. In these cases, even though the stock could go up and up and up like in our last example, investors like to spread out their buys over time. They don't want to make a single purchase, but would rather gradually get into the stock.

There are pros and cons to both approaches, but for this lesson, the takeaway is dollar cost averaging is a complex sounding phrase for simply investing the same amount of money into the same investment over a period of time.

64

WHAT IS SOCIALLY RESPONSIBLE INVESTING?

A vegetarian who owns McDonald's? Uh oh...

As a consumer, you vote every time you buy something. By buying this over that, you're effectively saying, "I support this company and not that company." A single dollar has little power, but when you are spending thousands of dollars in a year and millions of others are spending thousands of dollars in a year, consumers can cause companies to thrive or die.

Have you ever found yourself saying, "I'd never buy clothes from that store; all of their stuff is made in low-wage sweatshops." Or maybe, "I would never shop at that store because they don't treat their employees well."

Many people have strong feelings about the products they buy and the companies they support or don't support.

And just like there are consumers who don't want to buy things from certain stores they feel negatively about, there are investors who don't want to buy stock from companies they feel negatively about.

This is called socially responsible investing, or sometimes socially conscious or ethical investing. All are phrases for the same thing – investing in companies with the hope of making money but also doing social good. Or, on the flipside, *not* investing in companies who do social bad.

For example, I had a client who lost her husband to lung cancer. She was adamant she didn't want to invest any of her money in tobacco companies. She said she didn't want "blood money."

Another client, upset about the aftermath of the big BP oil spill in the Gulf of Mexico, didn't want anything to do with oil companies.

Another client, who is a pacifist and despises all things related to war and conflict, made it clear he didn't want any ownership of big defense companies who make planes, bombs, and tanks.

And still another client, this one a vegetarian, inherited a considerable number of shares of . . . guess what company? McDonald's! We couldn't sell these shares fast enough for her.

The goal with socially responsible investing is to do well by doing well; to make money and at the same time feel good about the companies you own.

For some investors, avoiding certain companies is important. They don't want to feel like they own something that goes against what they believe. For them, socially responsible investing is a way for them to be an investor, yet also stay aligned with their values.

Gordon Gekko definitely wasn't concerned with socially responsible investing

Critics of socially responsible investing will argue that as an investor, your goal should be to make the most money possible, and if that includes investing in some questionable companies, then that's what it takes. They'll also argue that many of the industries that are the most hated by socially responsible investors, industries such as oil, alcohol, tobacco, and defense, are also some of the most profitable and best performing areas in the stock market.

But socially responsible investors will say that as the public learns more about these industries, they will make better choices and that the companies which do well will also make more money as the public starts to vote with their consumer dollars.

65

REALIZED VS. UNREALIZED GAINS/LOSSES

Not as complicated as it sounds

There might be a few new words you will not be familiar with in this chapter, but trust me when I say you'll want to know what these mean. And sadly, many investors aren't even sure what they mean, but you will!

Let's party like it's 1999!

Stock	Buy Price	Current Price	Sale Price	Gain/Loss	R/U?
Pets.com	$10	$14	$14	$4 Gain	R
eToys.com	$30	$50	No way!	$20	U

A few months later…

Stock	Buy Price	Current Price	Sale Price	Gain/Loss	R/U?
eToys.com	$30	$1	$1	-$29	R

Take a look at the charts above. In the last column, the "R" stands for "realized." Realized means you have sold and you have locked in whatever gain or loss you have. Realized means you have really either made or lost money.

The "U" in the last column stands for "unrealized." Unrealized means you haven't sold yet, but if you did right now, this is what your gain or loss would be. Unrealized means you are still unsure when you are going to sell.

Who cares? Well, there may be some tax consequences that we'll talk about in a future lesson, but what's important here is that once you sell, you have locked in, or realized, your gain or loss.

When you sold the share of Pets.com for $14, you had $14 in your pocket. You could then take that $14 and buy the new Christina Aguilera single, *Genie in a Bottle*. Once you sold your share of Pets.com, you didn't care that the stock went from a high of $14 down to zip, zilch, zero. Didn't affect you because you sold and were *Livin' La Vida Loca* with Ricky Martin.

With an unrealized gain or loss, you still own the investment. You do care what happens because you still own it. As you saw with your share of eToys.com, you had an unrealized gain of $20, but you got greedy and didn't sell. Then a few months later, the stock plummeted and you eventually sold for $1 a share. You turned your unrealized gain you had into a realized loss. When you sell, you either realize a gain or loss. In this case, you bought eToys.com for $30 and sold it for $1, so you had a realized . . . loss. That's right.

Not so fast!

Quick story. Back in 1999, I get a call from a friend of mine. He's screaming in the phone, "I'm a millionaire, I'm a millionaire!" He tells me the internet company he works for gave him some stock in the company and the stock price was shooting up. He also said the company wouldn't let him sell it for six months. So, his stock really was worth millions. He had an unrealized gain. Unfortunately, like many internet stocks at the time, his company's stock dropped. When he could sell it, the stock was basically worthless. He went from having a million-dollar unrealized gain to having nothing. Some people refer to unrealized gains as paper gains. Why paper gains? Because you get your statement in the mail and on the statement it shows this big gain, but until you actually sell, the gain doesn't really mean anything.

Pop quiz. If I haven't sold an investment, is it realized or unrealized? It would be unrealized. As soon as you sell it, then it becomes realized. Is it a gain or a loss? That's easy. If you're selling it for more than what you bought it for, it's a gain. If you are selling it for less than you bought it for, it's a loss.

There it is. Realized and unrealized gains and losses. We like both realized and unrealized gains, but we don't actually have the money in our pocket until we convert those unrealized gains into realized gains when we sell, which is something I hope you do a lot of as an investor.

TECHNICAL VS. FUNDAMENTAL ANALYSIS

The Big Battle: Which Side Are You On?

In the investment world, this is like the rivalry between the NY Yankees and Boston Red Sox. I find that people are often in one camp or the other. And each will tell you why they are right and how the other group doesn't know what they are talking about.

The two camps are technical analysis and fundamental analysis. First of all, we have this word "analysis," but what is it exactly that we are analyzing? Turns out, we are analyzing investments. For what? Everyone is always trying to predict the future. They are trying to look into a crystal ball to predict what's going to happen with this investment or that investment. And can you imagine if you had a crystal ball that could tell you if a stock was going up or down? You'd be rich! And that's why there are so many people trying to find that crystal ball.

Stick to the fundamentals

Let's look at the fundamental analysts. These guys and gals have their own version of a crystal ball. For them, they try to figure out if a company's stock price will go up or down using fundamental analysis. This means they look at the fundamentals of the company. The fundamentals of a company are all about the inner workings of the company and the economy. They look at the company's revenue, expenses, assets, and liabilities. Is the company growing? Are they making a profit? Have they borrowed a lot of money? Can they pay it back? They look at the rate of employment in the economy and make projections based on all of these economic factors to determine if the company will do well or not. They look at the fundamentals of the company. Seems reasonable.

What about the technical analysts? What do they look at? The first thing they say is, "Who cares about the company's earnings and cash flow and all that other stuff? The real secret to predicting how the stock is going to perform has nothing to do with how the company has performed, but everything to do with how the company's stock has performed in the past." Huh?

What?

Technical analysts try to predict the direction of stock prices by studying patterns in what the stock price has done in the past. Their belief is that stock prices are really the result of humans buying and selling, that there is a certain degree of psychology with how humans behave and that stock charts visually show this psychology. They believe stock prices move in trends, again, because humans are humans and tend to act in similar ways given similar circumstances. And that if they can see patterns of what the stock did before, then they think those patterns or trends may occur again. They look at stock charts, which show how a stock has done over time, and try to see these patterns.

Technical analysts have all kinds of funny names for some of the patterns they see in these stock charts. Things such as head and shoulders formation, bullish abandoned baby, climax, and the inverse saucer among others.

If you've ever looked at one of those 3D *Magic Eye* books, or those 3D posters in the mall, and tried to see the image, you have a sense of technical analysis.

Both fundamental and technical analysts swear by their methods. And, of course, some investors use both. Most investors put more weight on the fundamentals of a company. If you are going to put your hard-earned money into a company, don't you want to know if the company makes money? If they owe a bunch of debt? I sure do.

As Warren Buffett famously once said, "I realized technical analysis didn't work when I turned the charts upside down and didn't get a different answer."

Stick to the fundamentals.

67

CORRECTIONS AND BEAR MARKETS: THE PROZAC CHAPTER

Warning. This chapter is for mature audiences only.
It may cause worry, sadness, and general malaise.

These next two chapters suck. I mean, the lessons are okay, but the content is awfully depressing. But we are all big boys and girls. As investors, we shouldn't kid ourselves. Let's have an honest look at what happens when things don't go as planned.

By the end of these lessons, you'll be familiar with all things bad when it comes to investing. You'll hear many of these words I'm going to talk about thrown around in news broadcasts and articles. Let's become familiar with them so they are not so scary.

The first two I'm going talk about, corrections and bear markets, relate to the stock market and how much stocks are going down.

What's a correction? First of all, what's with this term? When you hear "correction," don't you think that's something good? I mean, there was something wrong or off, and then there was this wonderful correction that came along and fixed it.

But, in the investment world, a correction is not a wonderful thing.

A correction is when the price of a stock, mutual fund, bond, or index, like the Dow Jones or the S&P 500, drops. But then they get fancy, and say, "Well, not just drops, but it has to drop by 10% or more." If the Dow Jones drops by 9%, then it's not a correction. If it drops 10.34%, then magically, we have a correction! It's kind of silly, but that's what it means.

A "correction" doesn't feel correct

But why do they call it a correction? The thinking is that the market or stock went up in value too much and that when it drops, it is really more in line with the real value. It's like a little kid running around and being crazy. You give the kid a timeout and then he calms down. That's the thinking, but it is ridiculous. A correction, really? It's just a nice way of saying, "Uh, you lost 10%, but don't worry, because now your investment is at the price it should really be at." Anyway, that's a correction.

Next what about bear markets?

You may remember that a bear market is one that what, goes up or down? Bears use their claws and strike down at their opponents. So a bear market is one that is going down. This is almost identical to a correction, but instead of the investment or index dropping by 10%, with a bear market, it has to drop by 20% or more.

So corrections and bear markets focus on how much the stock market is going down. Yay! How fun! But if you really want to be depressed, wait until the next lesson!

68

RECESSIONS AND DEPRESSIONS: THE MORE PROZAC CHAPTER

Warning. This chapter is also for mature audiences only. It may cause even more worry, sadness, and general malaise.

Just one more depressing lesson, and then we're done. I promise!

Things are not looking so good...

Next, we'll talk about recessions and depressions. Unlike corrections and bear markets, where these terms describe the stock market going down, recessions and depressions describe how much the economy is going down.

A recession is when a country's economy, meaning the goods and services produced in the country, takes a hit and declines. Let's make it a little easier to understand. Let's say you start a lemonade stand. Things are going great. You're making lemonade and selling as quickly as you can. You have a line of people waiting to buy your lemonade. This goes on for several years. Then, all of a sudden, the line gets shorter and fewer people want your lemonade. When this happens to countries, it's called a recession. A recession is when unemployment goes up and more people are out of work. Companies are not selling as much of their stuff. People are not rushing to the malls and filling their shopping bags. As a result, the total value of all goods and services produced over a month, or quarter, or year declines. That's a recession. It's when people, companies, and the country itself are not doing as well financially.

Could a recession lead to a stock market drop, such as a correction or a bear market? Yes, it sure could. But, a recession really only describes the drop in the economy and not the stock market. You could have a recession, but not a drop in the stock market. Just like you could have a correction or drop in the stock market without a recession.

Okay, now the big doozy. A depression. I get depressed just thinking about a depression. A depression really only applies to a single time in our country's history. It was back in 1929. The stock market crashed and everything went to hell in a hand basket. Usually, there is about 5% or 6% of our population looking for work. Back in the depression, 25% of the people were out of jobs and looking for work. Our economic sickness spread throughout the world. It was a bad time for people everywhere. People didn't have enough to eat. Not good. That was The Great Depression.

Okay, that's it! No more talk of depressions and bear markets. Only unicorns and rainbows from here on out!

69

WHAT DOES IT MEAN THAT A STOCK IS OVER OR UNDER VALUED?

Here's how to tell if you are buying a stock on sale or if you are over paying

Hey, do you want to buy my car for $8,000? You couldn't possibly answer that question without knowing more about my car. What is the make? Model? Year? Miles? Does it run? You get it.

The same is true for investing. You need to know something about the stock before you can decide if it's a good value or not.

Stick with me on this lesson. It's a little longer than most and there is a bit of math involved, but the payoff is worth it. You'll be able to answer this question by the end: "What stock is cheaper? One trading for $50 a share or one trading for $200 a share?" Of course, the answer will surprise you.

Here is how professional investors determine if a stock is a good deal or not: it's called valuation.

They want to know, "If I buy a share of stock in this company, what am I really getting in return?" It all comes down to how much money the company is making, called the profit. How much money do they make after all of their expenses?

Remember we talked about how owning a share of stock in a company is really owning a part of the company? I guess it would also be important to know how many total shares the company has. For example, let's say you owned a single share of stock in each of these companies:

Big, Inc.

Total Shares: 100 shares

Your Shares: 1 share

Your Ownership: You own 1% of the company

Small, Inc.

Total Shares: 10 shares

Your Shares: 1 share

Your Ownership: You own 10% of the company

Okay, so that tells us something. It tells us how much of the company we own. But it doesn't tell us everything yet. Think about it. Would you rather own 10% of my part-time babysitting business, or would you rather own 1% of Google, Home Depot, or American Express?

Why would you want *just* 1% of Google, when you could have 10% of my babysitting business? Because Google is huge and makes billions of dollars, and my babysitting company sucks.

That's exactly right. Google makes billions of dollars (almost $20 billion a year!), and my babysitting business makes hundreds of dollars a year.

Okay, we're getting somewhere now. It's not just how much of the company you own, but it's also how much money the company makes that's important.

If only there was a way to figure how much earnings the company makes for each share of stock they have. Something where you could figure out the earnings for each share. Something like earnings per share. Fortunately, there is an easy way to figure that out, and it has this awesome name that's really cool and exciting. It's called *earnings per share*.

Now let's have another look at our companies.

Big, Inc.

Total Shares: 100 shares

Total Earnings: $100

Total Earnings per Share: 100 shares/$100 = $1 of earnings for each share (EPS)

Small, Inc.

Total Shares: 10 shares

Total Earnings: $100

Total Earnings per Share: 10 shares/$100 = $10 of earnings for each share (EPS)

Hey, hey, hey! What do we have here? Our so called Small, Inc. company isn't so small now, is it? For every share you own of it, you get $10 of earnings. I like it!

Okay, just one last step here. Think how far we've come. We learned it's important to know how many shares there are of a company, as well as how much money the company makes.

Now we just need to see if it is a good value or not. If I said, "I have this great 2015 Porsche 911 with only 300 miles and it's in perfect condition, do you want to buy it?" what's your first question going to be? What color is it? No! You're going to ask, "How much are you asking?"

And that's the final step. How much is one share of stock in the company? Once you know that, you can see if the stock is a good value with a quick and easy calculation called the P/E Ratio. It sounds complex, but it's just taking the price of the stock and dividing it by the earnings per share. Here's how it works.

Big, Inc.

Total Earnings per Share: 100 shares/$100 = $1 of earnings for each share (EPS)

Price of the stock: $50 a share

Price/Earnings Ratio: $50 share/$1 EPS = 50 P/E

Small, Inc.

Total Earnings per Share: 10 shares/$100 = $10 of earnings for each share (EPS)

Price of the stock: $200 a share

Price/Earnings Ratio: $200 share/$10 EPS = 20 P/E

So Big, Inc. has a PE Ratio of 50, which means even though the stock price is just $50 a share, because there are so many more shares, each share gets just a small slice of the profit of the company.

On the other hand, Small, Inc. has fewer shares, and it only has to spread its profits to a small number of shareholders. So even though the stock per share is $200, you are getting a lot more profits per share.

The higher the PE Ratio means the less profit you are getting for each share of stock you are buying. So, the higher the PE, the higher the valuation, and the lower the PE, the lower the valuation.

As an investor, you will hear talk about valuations of a stock or the stock market as a whole is undervalued or overvalued. They are talking about the PE Ratio and how the current PE Ratio compares to their competitors and how it compares to itself over time.

For example, if the PE Ratio of UPS is 20 and the PE Ratio of FedEx is 100, that should cause some pause. They are both in the same industry. Why is FedEx so overvalued at 100 compared to UPS at 20? Or maybe, looking at it differently, why is UPS so undervalued compared to FedEx?

Whew! This chapter was a bit math heavy. Sorry! The takeaway? You can't tell if a company is over or undervalued based on the price of the stock alone. A $50 stock might be much more "expensive" and overvalued compared to a $200 stock. You have to look at earnings and the amount of earnings for each share.

70

VALUE VS. GROWTH INVESTING: WHAT'S A VALUE COMPANY?

This is the obligatory Warren Buffett chapter

You've probably heard of Warren Buffett, right? He's one of the richest people in the world. What makes Warren so interesting is, unlike the other richest people on the list who started companies, like Bill Gates (Microsoft), Mark Zuckerberg (Facebook), or Jeff Bezos (Amazon.com), Warren made his money through investing.

That's an amazing achievement. And you'd imagine it would be nice to know just how he made so much money ($75 billion, by the way) as an investor.

Well, you can, actually! The way he thinks about investing and the way he evaluates an investment is called value investing. There are countless books and entire college courses on just this subject.

So what is value investing?

It's an attempt to find the "diamond in the rough," the company that may have fallen on hard times and is not the prettiest girl at the dance. It's a solid company but is just a little rough around the edges. As a result, the stock price is not as high as it once was or as high as its competitors. Value investors look for good companies that are temporarily on sale.

Or a value stock may be an older and more mature company that just doesn't have the wow factor anymore. It's not growing as much as it used to, but it still has lots of customers and produces a lot of revenue. It's not the sexy high growth company it used to be. It's now just chugging along, doing its thing, making money.

Some investors like this kind of company. They like that it's a more mature company that has been around a while. They don't mind that it's not growing like crazy anymore. They're more interested in slow and steady growth from a company that is producing a consistent profit.

In fact, let's talk about companies and the money they make. If you're the president of a company and you're making a bunch of money, what could you do with this money? Well, if you are eTrade, you could spend $2 million on a Super Bowl commercial that featured a monkey dancing to La Cucaracha. Or maybe you could hire more employees. Or maybe you could use that money for research into a new product. Or maybe you could give some of the cash to the owners of your company, the stockholders. You could do any or all of these if you wanted.

But what should you do? Well, here's where it gets interesting. The big question is: what is the best use of this money? For some companies, they think the best use of the money is to reinvest it in their own company by trying to get more customers through advertisements, or producing more products, or getting more highly skilled employees to help the company grow.

On the other hand, some companies are so mature that they think the better use of this money is not reinvesting it in the company – we have enough money, and if we tried to grow, we'd just be wasting the money – so instead, they send some of that money to the stockholders.

The company that sends the money back to shareholders, the one that is more mature, stable, predictable, and is not growing as fast, is called a value company. As a value investor, you'd look for these types of companies to invest in.

Value companies send money back to shareholders

What are some examples? Coca Cola. Johnson & Johnson. Disney.

But why are value company stocks more stable and tend to be less risky? Well, again, they tend to be more mature. They've been around longer. They tend to have "better balance sheets." What does that mean? A balance sheet simply lists what a company owns and what a company owes. A "better" balance sheet means it owns a lot and owes very little. A value company may have more cash on hand. All of these things mean that if the economy declined and people generally slowed their buying, a value company with all that cash and experience might do better than a younger company with less cash and experience.

If that's a value company, what's the opposite? An un-value company? An anti-value company? Nope. It's a growth company. Well, that sounds quite dazzling. Growth. Who wouldn't want that? Lucky you. You get to learn about growth companies in the next lesson.

71

VALUE VS. GROWTH INVESTING: WHAT'S A GROWTH COMPANY?

Buying a value stock is good, but you don't want to miss out on growth stocks!

Are you feeling good about value companies? Remember, those are companies that seem to be undervalued, maybe because of a temporary setback, or companies that are more mature and stable. These companies tend to produce a lot of profit and might be more stable, but they are not expected to grow like crazy.

Growth companies reinvest their profits

Let's compare a value company with a growth company. Here's what you're getting with a growth company. Typically, growth companies take all the cash they make, and they dump it back into the company so it grows even more. They are not interested in giving their profits to shareholders. No way. They think they can do much better with the money by researching new products, advertising, trying to get new customers, and simply growing the company.

When a company starts, it's a growth company. It's small and trying to get customers and get bigger. But even some older companies are considered growth companies. Companies such as Amazon.com. It's been around for over 20 years, but it still takes the money it makes and plows it back into the company so it can grow even more.

Because investors like growth, these growth companies tend to have a higher valuation, meaning they are more expensive than other companies. So, there can be more risk with growth companies.

Most investors are not growth or value investors; they are growth *and* value investors. They use a combination of the two investing styles in their portfolio because there are times when the market, meaning the majority of investors, favors one style over the other. When this happens, you see a divergence between the two types of companies. For example, back in the late 1990s, almost all investors couldn't get enough of growth stocks. They loved growth stocks. More stable, mature, value companies? No way! High growth stocks? Oh, yeah. Bring 'em on!

So you had growth stocks do really well for a period of time. And then they didn't. Then after the dot-com crash, people were like, "I just lost a bunch of money. Who cares if a company grows fast? All I care about is stable and predictable returns. All I care about are value companies." Yes, just like that, you had the whole investment community, who days earlier loved growth stocks and disliked value stocks, completely shift their mindset.

As an investor, you will probably have both growth and value stocks. But when you look at your asset allocation, it's important to see what percent of your stocks are growth versus value. If you notice that 90% of your stocks are growth and only 10% are value, you'd better have a good reason if Warren Buffett asks.

WHERE SHOULD YOU INVEST? DIRECTLY WITH A MUTUAL FUND COMPANY

This can be a good option for some...

The question here is *not* "<u>What</u> should I invest in?" but instead, "<u>Where</u> should I invest?" You probably want to know your options, don't you?

One option is to invest with a mutual fund company. What's a mutual fund company? It's a company that has created at least one mutual fund that investors can invest in. Most mutual fund companies have not just one, but possibly hundreds of different mutual funds they've created that you can invest in. And all these mutual fund companies compete with other mutual fund companies to try to get investors to invest in their fund instead of their competitor's fund. I could start the Robert Mutual Fund that invests in U.S. large cap stocks. But maybe my neighbor gets wind of this and thinks he could do a better job investing in U.S. large cap stocks. So he starts the Joe Mutual Fund, and now we're both trying to attract investors into our mutual fund. There are hundreds of mutual fund companies that have created mutual funds and are all trying to get your investment dollars.

So, one option is for you to invest your money with a particular mutual fund company. For example, you may have heard of Vanguard. They are a company that provides mutual funds to clients. You can buy these mutual funds directly with them. You would just open an account by going to vanguard.com. You would then deposit money into your new Vanguard account, and then you could invest in any of the mutual funds that Vanguard offers.

Let me ask you this, though. If you had an account at Vanguard, where they sell Vanguard mutual funds, could you buy shares of an individual stock? For example, could you buy shares of Nike through Vanguard? No. It's like going to a Honda car dealership and asking if you can test drive the new Toyota Prius. Not going to happen. The Honda car salesperson will be more than happy to let you drive a Honda Accord hybrid, but they don't sell Toyotas. Same is true at Vanguard. They have their own mutual funds. They are not going to sell individual stocks or their competitor's mutual funds. They will sell just their own funds.

So why would anyone want to open an account directly with a mutual fund company? Well, maybe you are a big fan of Vanguard mutual funds, and you don't ever want to buy individual stocks or bonds, and you don't ever want to buy a mutual fund from a different company. That could work. The advantage is when you buy a mutual fund directly through the mutual fund company itself, you don't have to pay a transaction fee, which can be $10, $20, $50, or more. That's certainly an advantage.

WHERE SHOULD YOU INVEST? WITH A BIG BROKERAGE FIRM

You'll be in good company, but is it right for you?

As an investor, you could also invest with a brokerage firm. Why is it called a brokerage firm? Well, they act as brokers. Meaning, they are middlemen and women who sit between you (the investor) and the investments.

Brokerage firms can be big firms, such as Merrill Lynch, UBS, and Goldman Sachs, and they can also be smaller firms. Either way, they are more than happy to open an account for you, hold your money, and help you buy and sell investments. At these firms, you will probably have an investment advisor assigned to you. You can buy investments through her. Typically, you can buy almost anything you want. For example, want 100 shares of Google? No problem. Want to buy a Vanguard mutual fund? Usually not a problem (although some brokerage firms don't offer all mutual funds). Want to buy some bonds? Again, no problem.

Sounds perfect, right? And for many, this is a reasonable way to invest. With any option, there are some advantages and disadvantages. The disadvantages with going through a brokerage firm are:

1. **Fees**. They are the middleman. They don't get up each day and go to work for free. They do it to make money. And that's where you come in. If you invest with them, you will pay them any number of fees and commissions, and these can add up.

2. **Conflicts**. You'd think the advice you get from your investment person at a brokerage firm would have to be in your best interest, right? Well, sadly, that's not the case. Brokerage firms only need to provide you with advice that is "suitable," but not necessarily in your best interest. So who's

best interest could their advice be in? Who could it be? Uh, maybe the brokerage firm's best interest? Bingo! So that's definitely something to consider. Ideally, the financial advice you get would be entirely in your best interest – I mean, that just makes sense to me. If you are getting a recommendation, you don't want to think in the back of your head, "Is she suggesting this because it will benefit me, or is she suggesting this because it will benefit her?"

You'd be in good company if you invested your money through a brokerage firm. They work with millions of clients and have trillions of dollars in assets. Just know how they work and what you're getting into.

WHERE SHOULD YOU INVEST? RIA

The choice with the least conflicts of interest

One option as an investor is to invest your money with and through an RIA. An RIA is a Registered Investment Advisor. What's so significant about an RIA? An RIA is a financial firm that can advise clients about their investments, insurance, and general financial planning topics.

Some RIAs only act as advisors to your money, meaning you may have your money actually held at another firm.

For example, here is a common arrangement. Let's say your friend is an investment advisor and works for an RIA. You want your friend to help you with your investments. Here's what typically would happen. You would have an agreement with your friend's company, the RIA. The agreement would say something like, "We're an RIA and we will help you invest your money. We are responsible for researching and buying investments, etc. In return, you will pay us a fee."

So far so good. But then when it comes time to transfer your money so they can invest it, they will say, "Don't transfer the money to us. Instead, transfer it to a company such as Charles Schwab or Fidelity." This might be confusing to you. "I thought you were going to invest it for me. Why would I transfer it to Charles Schwab?" Many independent RIAs do not actually hold client's money, or what is called custody. They instead work with companies such as Charles Schwab, Fidelity, and others who hold the money but allow the RIA to have access to the account so they can make trades for the client.

Keep in mind that RIAs are in the business of what? Making money. Yes, of course, they are in the business of helping you make money, but they are also in the business of making money for themselves. They get compensated for their services. Just because you hear

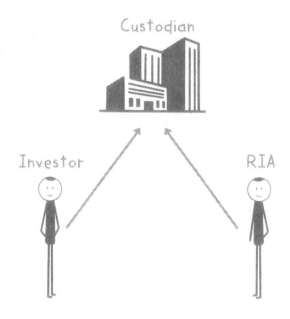

Custodian

Investor

RIA

Investing with an RIA is likely a good option for you

"RIA" doesn't mean they don't get commissions. Unless they are a "fee only" RIA, there could be commissions. RIAs could also charge a flat monthly fee or often a fee based on the size of the assets they manage for you, something called an asset under management fee.

One difference between RIAs and brokerage firms gets back to what we talked about in an earlier chapter. Brokerage firms must provide advice that is suitable for each of their clients, but the advice doesn't necessarily have to be in the client's best interest. With an RIA, this is different. An RIA must provide advice that is in the client's best interest. They are called fiduciaries. They have to do what is right for their client every single time.

The takeaway? An RIA is a firm that helps clients invest their money and can provide financial planning for a fee. Some RIAs hold the money, or custody, themselves, while others partner with a bigger firm to hold the money.

Investing with an RIA is a growing and popular option and will probably be a good option for you.

WHERE SHOULD YOU INVEST?
DISCOUNT BROKERAGE

Good for the DIY investor…

A discount brokerage firm is another way you can invest your money. A discount brokerage firm is a DIY approach. Here, won't need an advisor to work with you. Instead, you are going to be able to research and buy and sell stocks, bonds, mutual funds, and ETFs yourself.

If I need to change the oil in my car, I have a couple of options. I can take it to a Jiffy Lube or maybe the car dealership and get it serviced. Here, I'm paying for someone to do the job for me. Or, if I'm good with cars and don't mind spending some time and getting a little dirty, I could change the oil myself.

If someone does it for me, I'm probably going to pay more than if I did it myself. And this is the big draw with using a discount brokerage firm. It's the least expensive option because you are doing it yourself.

But, it's not called a "free" brokerage. It's a discount. That means there are still some fees involved. Just like if I wanted to change my own oil, I'd still have to buy the oil and would probably have some fees to get rid of the dirty oil. It's less expensive than Jiffy Lube, but there is still a cost.

Usually, the cost is when you buy or sell an investment. For example, if you want to buy 100 shares of Toys R Us, you might pay anywhere from a flat $8 fee to maybe $50. Yes, there is a cost, but in some cases, it is much less than if you used a brokerage firm or an RIA.

If you enjoy investing and think you would be good, it's certainly an option that puts you in total control and is less expensive.

Some common discount brokerages you may have heard of are Charles Schwab, Fidelity, and eTrade.

So what's a discount brokerage? A firm where you can deposit your money and where you make your own investment decisions and pay a fee whenever you want to buy or sell a stock or mutual fund.

SPEND SMART

Section 4

76

WHY WE BUY

The psychology of spending money

Why do we buy what we buy?

Maybe you have to have a $2,000 Gucci purse. Maybe this is a must-have for you. You wouldn't possibly carry around something less regal than this. Why? Is the Gucci purse better at carrying your wallet, cell phone, and Advil? Do less expensive purses have holes? Do the straps break? Are we to believe a $20 purse cannot effectively hold your stuff as well as a $2,000 purse? Are the Italians somehow superior when it comes to folding a piece of leather and adding a strap?

Functionally, a purse is a purse. The difference? A Gucci purse is beautiful and a $20 purse looks like crap. But why does that matter?

Here's why. We buy because of how it makes us feel. Period. End of story. We may feel better about ourselves carrying an expensive purse. We may see others looking at our expensive purse in envy and feel good about ourselves. We buy because of how it makes us feel.

If you were stranded on a remote island by yourself, would you care what kind of purse you had? We buy based more on feeling and less on function.

So what's the big deal?

It usually isn't a big deal, but sometimes we can overextend ourselves, financially buying stuff that makes us feel good but that we can't afford. It's like the second glass of champagne on New Year's Eve. It feels good in the moment, but we wake up with a terrible hangover the next day.

Buying based on feeling is ephemeral. This is one of my favorite words, by the way. It rolls off the tongue so nicely. Ephemeral. It means short-lived and fleeting. The buzz or high we get from the purchase quickly fades and requires us to buy more and more. I've seen this countless times over the years with clients. The "dream" house just isn't big enough, new enough, or nice enough after a year, and the next dream house is bought. Wash. Rinse. Repeat.

Like most of what I've talked about in this book, there is a great benefit in awareness – just being conscious of why we buy can help us make better decisions and influence how we spend and what we spend on.

Your homework for tonight, and frankly, for the rest of your life, is to think about not what you want, but why you want what you want. Is there another way you can satisfy that need without having to spend?

And if you do buy something, do you really know how much it costs? It may have a price tag, but the true cost is a little different. More on that in the next chapter.

77

THE TRUE COST OF SOMETHING

A really expensive iPhone!

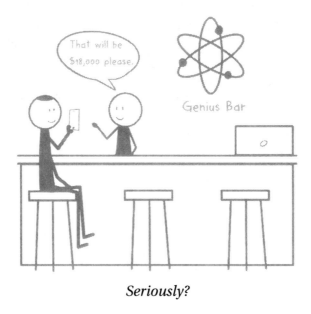

Seriously?

Have you seen the $18,000 iPhone? No? Think again. Hold up your smartphone. Are you looking at it? So not only have you seen the $18,000 phone, you bought one. Yup. That sucker you're holding cost you $18,000.

If the latest iPhone is on sale for $500, how much does it cost? What is the real cost of anything?

Instead of looking at the price tag and assuming that is what it costs, ask yourself how much you had to earn to buy it. What do I mean?

If you hand over five crisp $100 bills, what did it take for you to earn $500? Well, it wasn't $500. Remember that little thing called tax? For you to pocket $500, you really had to make over $800. Why? You may start with $800, but after federal income tax, state income tax, and payroll taxes totaling $300, you actually only get to keep $500.

So already that $500 iPhone cost a whole lot more than $500. At this point, it cost $800 or more. Okay, I know what you're thinking: $800 is a lot for a phone, but it's not $18,000.

Fair enough. Let's keep going. What would happen if instead of buying the phone, you invested in your company's 401(k) account? Something interesting. Because the money you invest in a 401(k) is not taxed, you could take that $800 you earned and invest it. Over time, that $800 could grow and grow and grow until it reached, yup, you guessed it, $18,000.

I'm not saying you shouldn't buy a phone, but I do want you to start thinking of these two things:

1. What did I really have to earn to buy this?

2. If I didn't buy this, what could this money grow to if I invested it?

Sometimes we think we want something, but if you can pause a moment and think about what you could do if you didn't buy it, you may, even once in a while, decide that whatever you thought you wanted is not worth it. And if you do that just a few more times a week or month, it can really make a huge difference.

So if you're going to be buying $18,000 cell phones, wouldn't it be nice to learn a simple strategy to cut your expenses? And wouldn't you know it, that's coming up next!

78

HOW TO CUT YOUR EXPENSES WITH PERK

They loved this on Good Morning America

No, honestly. *Good Morning America* loved what I'm about to share with you so much, they had me back three times. Why did they like it? Because it's an easy and painless way to cut your expenses.

All you have to do is PERK. No, I didn't say twerk. I said PERK.

Make a list:

The first step is to list all of your routine living expenses and upcoming expenses, from groceries and the cable bill to health insurance and property taxes. Flip through old credit card statements and checkbook registers for reminders, categorizing your expenses as you go. You don't need to have dollar amounts for each category; just the categories themselves should be enough.

Then, next to each expense, write a "P," "E," "R," or "K."

Postpone

For those expenses you are able to Postpone, you write a "P." Expenses in this category could include buying a new car, remodeling a kitchen, installing new carpet, or incurring a smaller expense, like buying a new TV or upgrading to the new iWhatever.

Postponing an expense gives you more money today so you can save or invest it. Plus, it helps avoid impulse purchases. Often, if you postpone a purchase for a few months, you are less inclined to make that purchase when the time comes.

Eliminate

Look for expenses you can eliminate, such as magazine subscriptions, newspaper subscriptions, Netflix charges, or unused gym memberships, and write an "E" next to them.

This is really where you want to spend as much time as possible. These are expenses that made a lot of sense at one point but don't anymore and probably haven't in a while.

Reduce

Look at each of your expenses and ask, "Is it possible for me to reduce it?" If so, write an "R" next to them. You can often slash the money you spend on restaurants, movies, cell phone bills, and groceries. Bring a brown bag lunch two days a week and you can save thousands of dollars.

Keep

And finally, some expenses are must-haves, like health insurance, auto insurance, mortgage payments, and rent. Mark these with a "K."

That's it. What makes this so effective is that it forces you to evaluate each of your expenses. You may find that you are spending money on stuff you don't even want, need, or like anymore. PERK helps you become more conscious about your spending, but I bet you want more unique money saving ideas. I bet you want to look at spending in a whole new way. Well, wouldn't you know it, you can.

79

A FEW TRICKS TO REDUCE YOUR EXPENSES

Painless strategies anyone can use

Here's a riddle for you. What's hard to get but easy to lose? A girlfriend in high school. Sorry, too personal. The real answer is money, of course! Here's a couple of tips I shared on CBS that may help you cut back a bit without even noticing.

1. **Don't budget**. I know, I know. All financial advisors say you have to budget, but I'm not one of them. Why? Budgets work, but no one likes them because they are hard to create and even harder to stick to. The solution? PERK instead! As I described in the last chapter, it takes about 15 minutes and can save you $250 to $1,000+ a month. Quick recap. First, list all of your expenses – everything. Then, next to each expense write a "P," "E," "R," or "K." For those expenses you can "Postpone," put a "P." For those expenses you can "Eliminate," put an "E." For those expenses you can "Reduce," put an "R." For those expenses you must "Keep," put a "K." Don't let the simplicity throw you. It's easy but incredibly effective.

2. **Stop leaking money.** We spend money on stuff we don't need or even realize. Things like cable channels we don't watch, subscriptions we don't read, and organizations we don't care about. Take a close look at where your money is going by using a free online program, such as Mint.com, to track expenses easily. Cancel all expenses you don't use or don't need.

3. **Create a buying buffer zone.** The goal is to create a buying buffer zone of at least 30 days between the moment you want to buy something (usually in the heat of the moment

A valuable buffer to cut back on expenses

at the store) and when you actually buy it. If you force yourself to wait 30 days, you'll find that most of the time, you won't want it anymore. If you still do, it means you really do want it. So instead of whipping out your credit card, whip out your phone. Take a photo of whatever you want to buy and post it on your "buyer board" or Pinterest account. Write the date, the amount, and a short reason why you want it and how it will improve your life. After waiting the 30 days, see if you still can't live without it.

4. **Get real**. Fill in the blank: "The three most important things in my life are _____, _____, and _____." Usually, stuff doesn't make the list. It's important to get clear and conscious about what you value. Print this list, or even better, find photos that represent the three things you value (e.g., pictures of your kids), and put these photos in your wallet/purse. To make sure you look at them, put them in front of your credit cards. If you really want to get fancy, create a credit card condom. This is where you make a sleeve for each of your credit cards with a photo of what's really important to you – this ensures you have to see your values before you spend money (especially on stuff that doesn't match your values).

5. **Volunteer.** Get the focus off yourself, what you want, and what new thing you just can't live without, and onto others who are in real need. This is great therapy, and it doesn't cost you a dime.

CREDIT CARDS ARE FREAKIN' AWESOME!

The financial planner police won't like this...

You heard it here first!

The problem with credit cards is . . . oh, who am I kidding? Credit cards are awesome! You know it. I know it. You know I know it.

Think about it. You get an idea for something you want. You don't have any money. You pull out this magical plastic card and the thing you wanted instantly becomes yours. This is better than a genie in a bottle! With a genie, you have to rub the lamp three times (who has the energy for that?), and you only get three wishes. With a credit card, it only takes one swipe and anything you want becomes yours.

How can you possibly compete with that? You can't. Credit cards are freakin' awesome. Really and truly. They are fabulous. And now with websites that send stuff same or next day delivery, you can just get an idea for something and buy it almost immediately. How? With a credit card.

Credit cards rock! If I've said anything but credit cards are awesome, you couldn't and shouldn't believe anything I've said up to this lesson.

Okay, so we agree credit cards are great. Yes? Excellent. My work is done. Almost...

FREE MONEY!
ALL ABOUT CREDIT CARDS

The gift that keeps on giving...

I'm so excited! I just bought a trucker hat, the *Nookie* Limp Bizkit album, *Gigli* movie tickets, and a Motorola StarTac flip phone. How cool is that? Yes, I'm aware that all this stuff was popular in the year 2000. But if you really need to know, I've been paying for this crap for almost 20 years and I just paid it all off!

Are you hearing the words that are coming out of my mouth? You could be paying off the stuff you buy today for the next 20 years. That's insane! Worse, you'll spend about twice as much. So if you thought it was a crime to pay 10 bucks to see *Gigli*, how would you feel knowing you really paid $20 to see it? Probably like a real loser.

What's the point? The early 2000s were a terrible wasteland for popular culture. No? I mean, yes, that's true, but no, that's not the lesson. We're talking about credit cards.

What can I possibly tell you about credit cards you don't already know? Take this quiz. Which of the following are true about credit cards?

1.   It can cost twice as much to buy something with a credit card after you pay interest.

2.   It can take over a decade to pay for something you buy today.

3.   Credit card debt can prevent you from obtaining real financial success and can suck the life from you.

4.   Average credit card debt is $5,047 and maybe not so coincidentally, 400 people are hit by lighting each year in the U.S. Connected? Do the math.

The unfortunate answer is that all of the above is true. So what have we learned so far? Credit cards are awesome. Credit cards will ruin your life and make you want to kill yourself. And credit cards cause lighting strikes. Perhaps that last one is a bit of an exaggeration.

So, what do we have here? A big fat mess. We have something we can't resist and that will provide us anything our hearts desire right now with something that will ruin us in the future.

What you need are some easy credit card rules to live by . . .

THE 8 CREDIT CARD RULES

This chapter can save your life…

If you're going to have a credit card, and really, what are the chances I'll actually talk you out of having a credit card, then please, at least practice safe charging.

You can avoid most of the dangers of credit cards by thinking about these credit card rules:

1. Admit you are powerless and weak. Don't delude yourself into thinking somehow you can avoid the siren call of the magic card. You can't and you won't. Don't rely on willpower. Instead, rule #1 is to promise you will follow these eight rules.

2. Only have one credit card.

3. Set the limit for how much you can borrow artificially low, like $1,500 or $2,500.

4. Pay off the balance every month.

5. If you find that you cannot pay off the balance in any month, immediately chop up the card and put a freeze on the account until you have paid off the balance.

6. Only buy things on the credit card that you know you can pay off at the end of the month.

7. If you find you are not able to control your spending, immediately chop up the card and close the account.

8. Pay on time each month. Don't ever miss a payment.

Seriously. People get into a lot of trouble with credit cards. And not a single one of those people thought they would when they started. It's okay. These rules take the guesswork out of it and will prevent you from digging yourself into too deep a hole.

AM I BEING TOO HARD ON CREDIT CARDS?

How to make $13 billion a year

I'm going to show you how to make $13 billion a year. Create a product that is irresistible, addictive, and just a little evil. Of course, you know what I'm talking about. Crack. Yes, I'm going to show you how to create a crack business.

You are going to make billions by giving crack to people, and then when they use it, you get paid. And here's the good part! If the crack user can't pay you in full each month, that's cool. You can still give them more crack. They will just owe you money and some interest. Okay, who am I kidding? They will owe you a lot of interest. But your customers won't care because they still are getting crack from you. They're happy for now. And if they start using too much crack and are having trouble paying you back? This is the best part. They are locked into the crack agreement. It is rock solid (pun intended). Sue them and put a lien on any future income they make. The crack business is a winner. Oh, sure, do you ruin some lives? Of course, but they had free will. They chose to do crack. Well, yes, you mailed them crack nearly every week and you put crack offers in their textbooks. But you didn't force them!

Credit cards are just as addictive

Oh, what's that? I'm so embarrassed. Have I been saying crack this whole time? I didn't mean for you to start a crack business, what I actually meant was for you to start a credit card business. How embarrassing that I mixed up the two! My sincerest apologies.

Am I being too harsh on the poor credit card companies that only make $13 billion a year? I was on a *20/20* episode several years ago. Also featured on that show was a lowly professor named Elizabeth Warren (I wonder what ever happened to her?). She said, "Credit card companies have a special word for the customers who pay in full every month. They're called deadbeats."

Why deadbeats? Here's how Visa makes over $13 billion a year:

1. **Transaction charges.** Every time you buy something with a credit card, the company selling you that something has to pay the credit card 2% to 4%. So if you buy a new iPhone for $500, Apple pays Visa $20 of the $500. Visa is making money with every swipe.

2. **Interest charges.** This is where they really make their big bucks. If you buy stuff but don't pay off your credit card bill, Visa is happy to let you pay off the balance over time. In return, though, they will charge you interest. That interest might be 5%, but more likely, it will be 15%, 20%, or even 25%+. Every day you don't pay off your Visa bill, you are getting hit with a very high interest rate charge. This is why it can cost you twice as much for that iPhone and why it can take so long to pay it off. As Elizabeth Warren says, credit cards don't want you to pay off your bill. They like it when it takes months, years, and even decades to pay off your bill because they get to collect all that nice interest.

This is how Visa makes $13 billion a year. There is good money in giving people what they want and then charging them twice as much for years to come.

We've learned that credit cards are magnificent and evil at the same time. It's hard to get around without them. But at the same time, they are incredibly dangerous and expensive. Sounds like a bad relationship I once had. And that's pretty much what credit cards are.

They are a very bad and abusive relationship. So, if you can resist, great! That's definitely the way to go. It's too easy to get sucked into the *buy now and pay later* trap. Every swipe of the card is a deal with the devil.

So, what's worse than using a credit card? I guess it would be using a credit card to buy crack. Try to avoid both.

WHAT'S YOUR CREDIT GPA?

Cs and Ds may get degrees, but a bad credit score gets you higher fees

Imagine being just one class away from graduating and having the professor tell you that passing the class all hinges on taking one final exam. "No problem!" you think. You're good under pressure. But then she tells you that you won't have any idea what the test will be about. That's not pressure. That's insanity!

But fortunately, credit scores are nothing like this. Say you had a few credit cards and were thinking about closing a couple as a way to improve your credit score. No problem. A quick Google search should inform you what to do. One of the largest credit scoring companies is kind enough to have an article on their website titled, "Improve Your Credit Score." Let's see what clear and understandable tips they have for us:

"Simply closing two accounts not only lowers the number of open revolving accounts (which generally will improve credit scores), but it also decreases the total amount of available credit. That results in a higher utilization rate, also called the balance-to-limit ratio (which generally lowers scores)."

After reading this simple explanation from the credit scoring company, I have a simple three-letter response for you: WTF?!?!

And welcome to the world of credit scores.

Trying to figure out what goes into a credit score is like asking Marshawn Lynch what he thought of the game.

Here's what we do know about credit scores:

- Your credit score is a number that is supposed to represent your credit worthiness and your ability to pay back debt.

- There are several different companies that provide credit scores.

- The more popular companies issue a credit score within the range of 300 and 850.

- The higher your credit score, the better your credit worthiness.

- Your credit score can change over time.

- Credit cards, banks, and other lenders rely a great deal on your credit score to determine if they want to lend you money.

- More and more employers check credit scores before they hire.

So what's the big deal about your credit score? A low credit score is no bueno. If you have a lower credit score, credit cards and banks may still lend you money, but they may not lend you very much and/or they will charge you a higher interest rate. Over time, you could easily pay several hundred thousand dollars more. Insurance companies may jack up your premiums if you have a low score. And that's not all! A low credit score can prevent you from getting a job.

Getting stuck with a low credit score really sucks. It's the modern day *Scarlet Letter*, but in this case, you get screwed after being branded.

Wouldn't you like to know how your credit score is calculated? Well, you're going to be in for a very big surprise in the next chapter.

HOW YOUR CREDIT SCORE IS CALCULATED

This may surprise you…

Houston, we have a problem.

The title for this lesson is, "How Your Credit Score Is Calculated," but here's what we don't know … how your score is calculated. Yeah, that's kind of a big deal. If you are going to be graded and so much lies on getting a good grade, wouldn't it be nice to know what you need for a good score?!

It probably seems like you have little control over your credit score, but that's not really true. Even though we don't know exactly how it is calculated, we do have some rules of thumb from credit scoring companies you can live by that will help improve your score:

1. Pay your bills on time. Late payments and collections can have a major negative impact on a credit score.

2. Keep balances low on credit cards. High outstanding debt can affect a credit score.

3. Apply for and open new credit accounts only as needed. Don't open accounts just to have a better credit mix. It probably won't improve your credit score.

4. Pay off debt rather than moving it around. Also, don't close unused cards as a short-term strategy to improve your credit score. Owing the same amount but having fewer open accounts may lower your credit score.

But there's one more powerful tool we have that can help us quickly improve our credit score …

A TRICK THAT CAN SAVE YOU $400,000

Who am I kidding? This chapter is going to be boring . . .

We have two competing issues. On the one hand, talking about credit reports is mind-numbingly boring. On the other hand, talking about credit reports can save you several hundred thousand dollars. I mean, don't get me wrong. I'm fond of money, but credit reports are sleep-inducing. It's your call. Skip ahead to the next lesson, or, if you can bear it, stick with me for just a minute and learn the least you need to know about credit reports.

If you're still reading this chapter, you are definitely a trooper. I think it's going to pay off for you.

Here's all you need to know:

- Your credit report shows information about you, such as where you live, if you pay your bills on time, and if you've ever been sued or filed for bankruptcy. This is the material the credit scoring companies use to help them figure out your credit score.

- There are three big credit scoring companies, and each of them has a credit report on you.

- You can get a free copy of your credit report from each of these companies every single year.

- There is a good chance there is an error on your credit report.

And it's this last one that can really bite you. A recent government study found that as many as 42 million people have an error on their credit report.

It's like studying your butt off all semester, acing the final, but getting a "C" in the class because the professor made a typo when calculating your grade. Getting a "C" when you deserve an "A" is bad, but paying an extra $400,000 in higher interest rates and insurance premiums over your life because of an error is just tragic.

Here's all you need to do:

1. Get your free credit reports by going to www.annual creditreport.com.

2. See if you notice any accounts that do not belong to you, charges or late payments that don't look right, or other issues you think are incorrect.

3. Dispute anything you think even looks remotely incorrect.

How do you dispute an error? That's easy, too. You send one letter to the credit scoring company and you send another letter to the credit card company, bank, or whoever it is supplying the bad information to the credit scoring company. Bam! That's it. And to make it even easier, our government provides a sample letter for each! You can go to http://moneysmartcourse.com.

Okay, so aren't you happy you stuck around for that? Yeah, I know. It's really hard to make credit reports exciting, but what this lesson lacked in creativity, whit, and entertainment, I'm hoping it made up in cold, hard cash for you.

87

THE TRUTH ABOUT DEBT

This is not what you want to hear...

Let's start with the basics. Debt is when you owe someone for money you have borrowed. Debt is really digging yourself a hole. The more debt you have, the bigger your hole. Instead of paying yourself first and saving for your own goals, you have to pay back the debt you owe. If the goal is to be financially free, independent, and on top of your own personal money mountain, you have to climb yourself out of the debt hole first.

The debt hole

Sometimes if you're in the debt hole for too long, it costs so much in interest that it's impossible to climb your way out. You get stuck in there. Your credit card bills are so high that all you can do is pay the minimum balance each month. But then the interest keeps racking up so you never can get to the point of paying it off. You get trapped by making just enough to survive but never enough to pay off the debt so you can save. That's the debt hole.

Debt sure sounds pretty horrible, and in most cases, debt is crushing, life destroying, and one of the worst financial decisions you can make in life. Scratch that last one. It's not just one of the worst *financial* decisions, it's one of the worst decisions you can make, period. Debt isn't just a financial problem. It becomes a life problem. A relationship problem. Talk to anyone who's had too much debt and they will tell you how it's affected their whole entire life, not just their credit score or their checking account balance. Their whole life has suffered as a result. When you have debt, you have a chain that prevents you from living fully. With debt, you may not be able to save for your kids' education. You may not be able to save for your retirement.

You may not be able to afford proper medical care. You may not be able to visit an ailing parent. You may not be able to start that business you've always wanted. You may not be able to spend quality time with your kids because you have to work two jobs just to get by. You may not be able to sleep well at night.

Listen up. Debt is no joke. Debt can rip the life from you. But is there such a thing as "good" debt?

GOOD DEBT VS. BAD DEBT

Is there a difference?

Okay, so debt generally stinks. I think we've established that in the last lesson. But sometimes you'll hear people talk about good debt versus bad debt. Is there really a difference, or is it just a scam?

What's bad debt? Where do I start? Actually, let's just assume that all debt is bad debt, unless it's good debt. Can we do that? So that means, unless the debt falls into the category of good debt, we can assume with a high degree of certainty it is bad debt and that it will ruin your life. Okay?

Will it increase in value over time?

So, what then is good debt? Remember we talked about assets? These are things that you own that have value, such as a car, new kitchen table, or mutual fund. We don't want to use debt to buy just any assets. We would only consider using debt to buy *appreciating* assets. And no, an appreciating asset is not an asset you are thankful for. An appreciating asset is one that appreciates, which means it goes up in value.

So, let's take a look at the examples from earlier. Which one might go up in value over time?

- Car

- Kitchen table

- Mutual fund

Out of all three choices, the only answer is the mutual fund. If you're strapped for cash, think twice before you purchase a new car or kitchen table.

The lesson here is that if you're going to go into debt, make sure it is for an asset that will go up in value over time. Ask yourself, "Am I buying something, or am I buying an investment?" If you're not buying an investment, then do *not* buy it with debt.

What are a few examples of good debt? Buying a house and having a mortgage. Over time, houses generally go up in value. That's a fair use of debt. Education could also be a good use of debt. Think about it. You are the asset in this case. If the education will help you get a designation, new degree, or new skills that will help you advance in your career and make more money, then *you* are the appreciating asset. But be careful here. Before you pull out your credit card, really think long and hard about what you are buying and if the class or education will really help you make more money. If not, it's just an expense and it's a bad use of debt.

Borrowing to invest in a business could be good debt, but be very careful. Just because you want or hope an asset will go up in value doesn't mean it will. Before you become a slave to debt, you must be sure whatever you are using the money to buy has a *very* good chance of going up in value. A business could go up, but many people have gotten themselves into trouble by borrowing too much, not seeing their business succeed, and then being stuck with a lifetime of bad debt dragging them down.

Want a quick rule of thumb when it comes to good debt and bad debt? Just ask yourself, "Will I make money by buying this?" If the answer is "Yes," it's good debt. If the answer is "Maybe," "I'm not sure," or "No," then it's bad debt. Stay away!

But what should you do if you are already in debt? I'm so glad you asked!

89

HELP! I WANT TO GET RID OF THIS DEBT!

Real strategies that work

Firstly, you rock. Listen, I get it. It's easy to get into debt. Having debt reflects past decisions. Today is a new day. And today, you want to pay it off. Congratulations for coming to that decision!

When you find yourself in a hole, the first step is to stop digging. That means chopping up your credit cards and putting a freeze on them so you can't charge more.

That's step one, but what if you have several credit cards, an auto loan, a house mortgage, and some student loans? Where should you start? This is where it could make a lot of sense to talk to a financial planner, but generally speaking, you want to tackle your credit card debt first.

In the financial world, there is a big debate when it comes to paying off credit card debt. Do you do the snowball approach and pay off the small balances first and then tackle the larger debt, or do you pay off the debt with the highest interest rates first?

The answer? They both miss the bigger point. If you have debt, good on you for making an effort to pay it down. The "how" is essentially meaningless. Pay off the smaller balances? Pay off the higher interest rate balances? Whatever. Don't focus so much on *how* you are going to pay down the debt each month, focus instead on *how much* you can pay down the debt each month.

Big difference. Huge difference.

Here's how you can pay down more of your debt each month:

1. Cut your expenses. Every dollar you don't spend is a dollar you can use to loosen the debt noose around your neck.

2. Make more money. Yes! Focus on how you can make more money. Second job? Overtime? Start a freelancing business? If you had to make an extra $100 a week, what would you do? No, really. If your life depended on it, and it does, how can you make an extra $100 a week? You could solve your problem in a fraction of the time by making a bit more money and using it all to slash your debt.

Remember, it's not about which strategy you use to pay off your debt; it's making the decision you are going to pay off your debt, cutting up your cards, and coming up with ways for you to pay down your debt more each month. That's how you become debt-free in record time. It's not the snowball approach; it's the freakin' avalanche approach.

90

SHOPAHOLIC SYNDROME: WHEN YOU JUST CAN'T STOP BUYING STUFF

Here's what I said about addiction to Dr. Drew

When it comes to beating a shopping addiction, shame and logic don't work

Alcohol, crack, and heroin are known to be highly addictive, but can something as innocuous as shopping be addictive?

Dr. Drew Pinksy is an addiction specialist. You may know him as just Dr. Drew. I've worked with him on a few TV shows. Here's what I said about shopping addictions on the *Ricki Lake Show* with Dr. Drew.

First, it's important to understand what doesn't work. A shopping addiction is not a disease of intellect; it's a disease of emotion. Unfortunately, most family members, along with mental health and financial "experts," make things worse by focusing on the two areas that usually lead to even more shopping: shame and logic.

What's wrong with you?! Don't you know better? How can you be so self-centered and selfish? All shame accomplishes is guilt followed by more shopping.

Trying to use logic – if you spend too much, you won't have money to make the car payment – tends to be just as ineffective.

Such "cures" don't work. Shopaholics already feel bad about themselves, and they already know they can't afford it. Criticism often leads to people feeling even more socially isolated, which they "treat" by shopping. So if you find that you are spending more than you can afford and you can't seem to stop, these suggestions might help:

1. **Identify the shopping trigger.** What activates a person's urge to shop – boredom, guilt, shame, anger? Keep a written journal or electronic record and document what leads to the shopping.

2. **Discover the need shopping fills.** Excessive shopping doesn't serve a functional purpose – you probably don't need 15 purses – it serves a psychological purpose. For the non-shopaholic, it may look like "crazy" or irrational behavior. It's not. The shopaholic is often entirely rational. They shop for a reason – it fulfills a need, so they keep doing it.

   So the first step in halting compulsive shopping is to identify the psychological need driving it. Does the shopping provide pleasure or does it help you avoid pain?

   In other words, do you shop to feel something you don't feel anywhere else throughout the day (a rush, excitement, variety, stimulation, being in control, feeling naughty), or do you shop to avoid feeling something negative, such as anxiety, loneliness, or fear? Determine what part of the shopping provides the reward. Is it going with friends (social)? Is it being around others (community)?

3. **Replace shopping with something healthier.** The shopaholic needs to find a healthier alternative to filling the need. Brainstorm how you could fill this need in other ways. Often, you'll find that someone with one addiction will trade it for another addiction. This is not a positive long-term solution. The goal is to trade in a negative and destructive addiction for one that is positive and healthy, or at least neutral.

4. **Change your environment.** Our environment plays a huge role in our behavior. If you keep a bowl of jellybeans on your

desk, it's clear what you will snack on throughout the day. Use the environment to your advantage. It makes no sense for the alcoholic to "test" their willpower by having a snack at their local bar, and it makes no sense for the shopaholic to be in shopping malls. Create "no-fly zones" – places you can't go, such as malls, stores, and other shopping areas. You want to remove any ambiguity in your rules. If you don't, then, in the heat of the moment, the shopaholic will rationalize a way to shop. Make a list of the places you can and cannot go. Eliminate any TV watching (at least in the beginning), and stay away from magazines and newspapers. You basically want to remove any cues from the environment to shop.

5. **Get support.** Kicking an addiction is hard to do alone. Get some help from friends, family, or a therapist. Debtors Anonymous is a great resource, and they have groups in cities across the country.

KEEPING UP
WITH THE CAPUCHINS

This is the story about two naughty monkeys

Your money is threatened by a Trojan horse that comes in the form of a wide grin, a wink, and maybe a hug. This threat is like a computer virus. It runs without your awareness, takes hold of your operating system, and undermines your intentions. This threat affects nearly everyone, myself included.

It's been said that we are the average of the five people we're closest to. If you're making $40,000 a year, and all of your friends are making $100,000, you tend to spend more than you can afford to match their lifestyle. You may start to buy the same types of clothes or the same kind of car. You might take up the same expensive hobbies or move into the same neighborhood. Contrary to what most financial advisers suggest, the biggest threat to creating lasting wealth is not your poor friends. It's your rich friends.

Such financial creep is hardwired within us. We are social creatures. We are constantly looking at others and learning and modeling from them. It's in our DNA through evolution and natural selection. Our ancestors who saw and learned from others about what worked and what didn't were the ones who survived. Animals do it, too.

Imagine two monkeys in separate cages. A researcher gives the first monkey a slice of cucumber. The monkey grabs this and starts to eat it because monkeys like cucumbers. The researcher then gives a grape to the second monkey. The second monkey devours it because, while monkeys enjoy cucumbers, they love grapes. The first monkey is looking but doesn't really think much of it. The researcher then gives another cucumber slice to the first monkey. The first monkey takes it a little more slowly and starts to eat it, but now he's watching the researcher and the other monkey more closely. The researcher then gives another grape to the second monkey. Again, the second monkey gobbles it up.

It's called relative deprivation

If you watch the first monkey, you can tell something is not right. He's trying to figure out why he's getting cucumber slices and his buddy is getting grapes. Finally, the researcher gives another cucumber slice to the first monkey. The first monkey takes it, looks at it, looks back at the researcher, and throws the cucumber slice through the cage, hitting the researcher right on the chest. This monkey is irate. He does not understand why he is stuck with cucumbers, while his friend gets grapes.

Just two minutes before, he was thrilled with his cucumber. And now he is enraged. Why? It's called relative deprivation. We're constantly comparing ourselves to those in our immediate circle and looking for areas where we're not getting what we think we deserve.

Let me give you a human example: Imagine someone who has worked hard for many years to buy a Porsche 911. He has finally saved enough to throw down $100,000 at the dealership and drive off in a new Porsche 911. The windows are down, the radio is up, and he's cruising. But when he drives into a parking lot, he pulls up next to . . . what? A fancier car? A faster car? A more expensive car? He gets out of the Porsche, shuts the door, and feels disappointed. It's an internal tug that whatever we have isn't quite good enough; that maybe we're not good enough.

This seriously threatens our finances. You know what's going to happen to the guy with the Porsche. In three months, he's going to sell it at a huge loss and borrow money to buy or lease a car that's much more expensive than he can afford.

This virus is almost impossible to delete. The best defense is awareness. The next time you buy something, ask yourself why you want what you are buying. Do you truly want it, or are you just buying it so you look better or to assuage an internal battle to feel good enough?

The takeaway is to be conscious of how your environment and those around you affect your motives. Use money to create a better, fuller, and richer life. Don't use money to attempt to keep up with friends or to mitigate feelings of inequity. It might not be fair that your friends enjoy grapes while you get cucumbers, but if you act like the monkey, you'll have neither grapes nor cucumbers to eat.

92

HOW MUCH CAN YOU TAKE FROM YOUR INVESTMENTS AND NOT RUN OUT OF MONEY?

Don't kill the chicken

So I'm 15 minutes into an explanation of what I think is a pretty important and complicated subject when my client stops me mid-sentence. She says, "So basically, don't kill the chicken." I pause. I pause some more. She looks at me like I'm an idiot, and I look at her like she's crazy. Guess who was right?

Imagine you just worked your last day. You are now officially retired! The smile on your face knowing you'll never have to work again quickly turns to a frown as you start to worry about paying your bills.

Let's say you have a portfolio with $1 million. It seems like a lot of money. How much can you take each year? Well, if you took $1 million a year, you'd be broke in just one year, but I'm sure you'd have one hell of a year!

Broke in a year doesn't sound like such a good retirement plan. What if you took $1 a year? Your portfolio would last at least 1 million years, right? But can you really live on just $1 a year?

Okay, well, what if you wanted to take some amount between $1 and $1 million a year? And that's the big question. A lot of times, someone will ask, "How much can I take out of my investments each year and not really risk spending down my portfolio?" If you're retired, the last thing you want is to run out of money. But at the same time, you'll probably need to take some money out of your investments to live on. The question is how much can you take out and be fairly safe that you don't spend down all your investments?

There are a lot of factors that go into the answer, including how your investments are allocated and your age. But, we have a pretty good rule of thumb when it comes to answering the question, "How much can I take out from my portfolio without it running out of money?"

The rule of thumb is the 4% rule. You can be fairly safe taking out 4% from your portfolio a year – sometimes more, but generally, it's around 4%. That means, you could take out $40,000 from your $1 million portfolio each year and be pretty confident that you will not run out of money.

Seriously though, don't kill the chicken

And that brings me back to my client and the chicken. My client explained, "Your chicken lays eggs. Those eggs are like income. If you try to get in there and get more eggs, you'll kill the chicken, and then she can't produce any more eggs for you." How cool is that metaphor? Your portfolio will produce for you, but if you spend it down, it can't keep up.

So, in the end, my client was right and I was the idiot. It was totally worth it, though, to hear her chicken and egg metaphor. It is a great explanation and I've used it ever since.

TAX SMART

Section 5

93

WHAT ARE TAXES?

It doesn't have to be complicated

If you've ever thought to yourself, "The hardest thing in the world to understand is income taxes," you may be a genius! You see, that little quote was said by the guy who brought us the theory of relativity, the one and only Albert Einstein. Yup, one of the smartest minds the human race has ever produced thought income taxes were challenging to understand. So, where does that leave the rest of us mere intellectual mortals?

Because taxes are usually everyone's biggest expenses, bigger than rent, insurance, food, etc., we need to have some understanding of what they are and how we can minimize them.

I think if Einstein were alive today, he'd approve this message.

Pop Quiz

Let's first talk about what a tax is. Pop quiz. Are taxes:

A) A nice and arbitrary gift you provide,

B) A compulsory contribution levied by the government.

If you guessed B, you're obviously correct. Let's break that down just a bit. Compulsory means you must do it. A tax is not a choice. It's a requirement. A tax is a must do. Levied by the government means the government is the group that is forcing you to pay the tax.

No one likes taxes, so why have them? Few would deny that taxes are necessary to pay for things the government provides. Where people argue is how much tax is reasonable and how the government spends the money. But generally speaking, whether you are a Democrat, Republican, or in between, they all agree that we need some tax to pay for our military, police, hospitals, roads, etc. All that stuff isn't free. It costs money to hire people to build a bridge and to buy the materials. Where does that money come from? Usually taxes.

So, taxes are a necessity and the government makes us pay them. Or as U.S. Supreme Court Justice Oliver Holmes said, "Taxes are what we pay for a civilized society." Of course, he could have added, "And to pay the salaries for U.S. Supreme Court Justices." Just for fun, guess how much a U.S. Supreme Court Justice makes a year? About $250,000. Good thing there are only nine of them!

Sick of reading about taxes? I mean, really, what's the big deal with paying a little tax? You're about to find out . . .

94

WHAT'S THE BIG DEAL WITH TAXES?

A math teacher didn't believe this calculation

You're learning a lot about taxes, but maybe you're not convinced taxes are a big deal. I feel ya. Maybe you're right. Maybe taxes aren't such a big deal.

Let's run through a quick little example. Imagine you had an investment that doubled in value every single year. First of all, that would be amazing! But let's say you had this investment. The first year, you start off by investing $1. By the start of the second year, you would have $2, then $4, $8, $16, etc. Let's say this doubling went on for 20 years.

Take a guess at how much you'd have invested at the end of 20 years? A cool million bucks!

But what does this have to do with taxes? Nothing yet. Patience. Okay, now let's add taxes. Let's say that every year there was a 33% tax on the growth in the account. Whatever money you had after taxes would still double each year.

Without the 33% tax, the account was over $1 million in 20 years. With the 33% annual tax, how much would the account be worth at the end of 20 years?

Well, 33% is a third, so most people guess about $700,000 or so, but that's actually a bit too high. Then people will say something crazy, like $500,000. But even that's a little too high. Can you see how taxes eat away at your wealth? Instead of being a cool millionaire at the end of 20 years, you have less than half that amount because of a 33% tax. And think about this: a 33% tax isn't even that high. The highest federal income tax is almost 40%, and that doesn't even include any state tax you might owe.

So, yes, taxes are a big deal indeed. If you aren't aware of them or aware of strategies to minimize them, you could be paying a lot more than you should.

Okay, so how much would the account actually be worth at the end of 20 years with a 33% tax on the growth each year?

$28,000

Don't believe me? It's true. You'd only have an account worth $28,000 at the end of 20 years. That's the power of taxation. It can rob you of your money and leave you with much, much less than you'd have otherwise.

Your goal shouldn't be to read all 80,000 pages of the tax code, or to even file your own taxes. Your goal should be to understand how insidious taxes are to building wealth and to make sure you have people on your team who are obsessed with minimizing your taxes.

Well, I guess the good thing is that there are only a couple of different kinds of taxes, right?

95

WHAT ARE THE DIFFERENT TYPES OF TAXES?

There are probably more than you think

Let's test your tax knowledge. What are the different types of taxes?

A) Bad

B) Not Good

C) Terrible

D) Rotten

E) Horrible

That's a little tax humor for you. I'm here all tax season. Don't forget to tip your tax preparer!

So, what are the actual different types of taxes? I hope you're sitting. There are quite a few: federal income tax, state and/or local income tax, unemployment tax, sales tax, foreign tax, value-added tax, estate taxes, capital gains taxes, property tax, excise taxes, luxury taxes, corporate tax, GST tax, carbon tax, windfall tax, Medicare tax, Social Security tax, alcohol tax, gas tax, and many others. It is taxing to talk about the many types of tax. That line kills with CPAs.

I'm going to talk about all the rules for each of these different taxes.

Okay, I'm just kidding. That would be ridiculous. You don't need to know the rules for each of these, but we're going to hit the big ones.

First, let's group them into categories so we can better understand them. Almost any tax can fit into just one of the following four buckets:

MAKE IT TAXES

Income taxes. You're probably already familiar with this one. If you make income from a job, from selling lemonade through your business, or from making money from other sources, you might experience an income tax.

Payroll taxes. These are taxes you pay that's usually from your paycheck for Social Security and Medicare.

Investment taxes. If your investments make money, and let's hope they do, you may have to pay tax on the gains. For example, if you earn interest or you get rent from someone renting your house, that's taxed! If you sell an investment for more than you bought it for, that's taxed, too, and is called a capital gains tax.

It's taxing to talk about the many types of tax

Taxes such as the income tax, payroll taxes, and capital gains taxes on the income your investments make all fit nicely in this bucket.

It's like when you open a can of tuna and your cat and all the cats in the neighborhood come running from out of nowhere. If you make money, the government perks up and becomes very interested.

SPEND IT TAXES

So the government wants a piece if you make it, and now they want a piece when you spend it? Three letters. Y-U-P.

The most common type of "spend it" tax is the **sales tax.** You buy a box of multi-grain steel-cut oats with flaxseeds cereal . . . who am I kidding? You reach for a box of Froot Loops for $3.99 but end up paying $4.25. That extra 26 cents is sales tax. Sales tax is determined by the state and city where you buy the goods. Some cities and states don't have any sales tax (shout out to Portland, Oregon) and others do (shout out to Birmingham, Alabama with a sales tax of 10% – ouch!).

When you fill up your gas tank, chances are the price per gallon you pay at the pump includes a bunch of taxes.

If you buy booze or cigarettes, again, chances are the price includes a lot of taxes.

OWN IT TAXES

If you own property, like land or a house, then you will most likely have to pay **property tax**. Fortunately, property here doesn't include your stocks and bonds. When I say property, I'm talking about real property. Houses, buildings, and the like.

GIVE IT TAXES

Many years ago, when I was learning about taxes, I just didn't understand this one. My professor said, if you give money to someone, you might have to pay a tax. Huh? How could this be possible? If I give money to a friend, then I might have to pay tax? How does that make any sense? Sense or no sense, it's called the **estate and gift tax**.

If you give too much money away while you are alive, you will have to pay a gift tax. If you give away too much money after you die, it's called an estate tax. If I were a wittier person, I'd be able to come up with a funny quip related to the old saying, "The only things that are certain in life are death and taxes," but alas, I'm not, so I won't.

Make too much, spend too much, own too much, or give away too much, and you will most likely have to pay tax.

What's the alternative? Don't make very much, don't spend very much, don't own very much, and don't give away very much? Or, just maybe, there are other ways to reduce the taxes you pay? Keep reading for more on this!

WHO DO I PAY TAXES TO?

You can make the check payable to...

A boy getting a cavity filled asks his dentist, "Mr. Dentist, do I need to floss my teeth?" The dentist stops what he's doing and replies, "No, definitely not. You only need to floss the teeth you want to keep."

And so it goes. Do you need to know about or care about taxes? Nope. But if you kind of have an affinity for money and somewhat of a desire not to be broke, then sure, I guess it makes sense to know a little about taxes.

But there are so many! Which ones should you know about? We can slash two buckets off our list because there's really not a lot you can do about them. Those two are the "spend it" taxes, like sales tax, and the "own it" taxes, like property tax. Again, not a lot to know or plan for with these taxes.

The bigger fish, the much bigger fish, are "earn it" taxes. Primarily, income taxes and investment taxes. For my clients, these taxes are their biggest expense, so it makes sense to know a thing or two about them and how to minimize them.

The other big fish for some people are the "give it" types of taxes, mainly estate taxes and gift taxes. I'll talk about these in a future lesson, but for now, let's focus on income taxes.

Income taxes are based on the income you make from your job or your business. There are two groups who tax your income:

1) Federal Government

2) State Government

Let's talk for just a second about state taxes and then move on to the big guy. Depending on the state you live and work in, the state may tax you on your income. So, if you live in California, you will have to pay the state of California tax on the money you make. Not that you asked, but guess how many states have no income tax? Just seven (Alaska, Florida, Nevada, South Dakota, Texas, and Washington).

Having to pay state income tax is no good, and the amounts they want can really add up, but the bigger fish to fry (or for you vegetarians out there, the bigger tofu to toast) is the tax you pay the federal government.

Have you heard of the IRS? This is the federal government organization that is in charge of calculating and collecting the income tax you owe. What does IRS stand for? Income Reduction System? Nope, just kidding – a little tax humor there. IRS stands for Internal Revenue Service.

Do not pass go.
Do not collect $200.

The federal government, through the IRS, makes you pay them some of the money you make. Oh, and if you don't pay them? You go to jail. You go directly to jail. You do not pass go. Just ask Wesley Snipes, who owed $17 million in back taxes and was sentenced to three years in prison.

WHAT IS ORDINARY INCOME?

An extraordinary lesson on ordinary income

Person A makes $100,000. Person B makes $50,000. Who is going to pay more tax?

Well, obviously the guy making $100,000 is going to pay a lot more tax than the guy making $50,000, right? Guess again!

Here's what's going on. Not all money is created equal. Not all money is treated the same in the eyes of the IRS. And this is a very BIG idea with ginormous repercussions. Think about it. If you can make $100,000 and pay less tax than your neighbor who makes $50,000, don't you want to know how you can do that?

So, let's get a feel for how the IRS looks at different sources of making money and how they tax each.

The good news is that there are really only three types of income to worry about. But honestly, I don't even like using the word "income" here, because when most people think of income, they think of working at a job and getting a paycheck. And yes, that is income, but some of these others don't require you working a job, so when I say "income," keep an open mind as to what this income is.

The first type of income the IRS cares about is called ordinary income. This is not to be confused with extraordinary income, which is reserved exclusively to describe Adam Sandler's salary for pretty much any movie he's ever been in. Okay, no. Not really. There is just ordinary income. What is this ordinary income of which I speak? It's almost any kind of income you can think of. Yes, it's the income you get from your job, but it's so much more. If you rent a room out in your house and get paid, this is rental income and is considered ordinary income. If you own a bond and receive interest, this money is considered ordinary income. If you babysit, that's ordinary income. If you have a company that makes paper mâché hats, this is ordinary income. If you write a book and I buy a copy from you, that's ordinary income. If your cat video goes viral on YouTube and you get money from ads, that money is ordinary income. Almost any income you can imagine is considered ordinary income.

So what's the significance of this? *You* may like to earn ordinary income, but the IRS really likes it when you earn ordinary income. Why? They tax it! They get a piece of it! The more you make, the more they get. And it gets worse.

Ordinary income is like pizza. The IRS loves it and will do whatever it takes to get some of it from you.

My daughter loves thick, cheesy pizza. If I only had one slice of delicious pizza, I may try to hide it from my daughter (don't judge me; it's pizza!). But sooner or later, she'd see me eating that delicious slice of pizza. She would ask, then beg, then cry, then sulk, then demand some of my pizza. How do I know her precise emotional response from pizza shunning? Yeah, don't ask.

Ordinary income is delicious cheesy pizza. The IRS knows you have it and will do whatever it takes to get some of it from you. And not just a little, but a lot. They love it and they want a good part of your slice. If you don't give it to them, they won't beg, cry, or sulk. They go straight to demanding it and then to locking you up in prison.

That's ordinary income.

Oh, and I lied. This isn't the least you need to know about taxes and investing. There's just one more lesson, I promise. Okay, fine. There are two more. That's it. No, really. You can trust me!

HOW ARE CAPITAL GAINS TAXED?

If you don't like how ordinary income is taxed, you'll love this chapter

In the last lesson, you learned what ordinary income is. Do you remember? It's basically income from most sources – work, rental income, whatever. I talked about how ordinary income is like pizza and how the IRS loves to get their hands on it. Are you with me? Is it coming back now?

Okay, forget pizza for a second. Now let's say my daughter strolls by as I'm eating a bowl of whole wheat pasta. Will she want some of mine? Yeah, sure. She'll have some, but she doesn't love it. There won't be any tears or begging. She'll eat a little and then move on. I mean, it's whole wheat pasta. It's okay, but it's definitely not pizza!

And this leads us to the next type of income in the eyes of the IRS. The whole wheat pasta of income. This income is called capital gains income.

To understand what capital gains income is, you first need to know what a capital gain is. Don't worry. You'll pick this up quickly. Here's an example:

You buy a house, bond, stock, or some kind of investment for $100 and then later you sell it for $125. The difference between the two is $25. That's called growth, appreciation, a realized gain, or a capital gain. It went up in value. See? Simple. And guess what, the IRS wants a piece of that $25 capital gain. That's why it's called a capital gains tax.

But we already said capital gains are the whole wheat pasta of income. These capital gains are not delicious pizza. So what does this mean for us? It means that the IRS wants a piece of that gain, but not as much as if it were pizza income – oh, sorry, I mean ordinary income. That means you pay less tax with capital gains than with ordinary income.

Pop quiz. Which of these requires you to pay *more* tax:

$25 from a job or a $25 gain on a stock you sold?

If you guessed the $25 from your job, you're correct!

Most people have heard of Warren Buffett, but have you heard the Warren Buffett Rule? If you're Warren Buffett, and one of the richest people in the world, you get to make the rules. No, that's not it. It's this: he's a pretty generous fella. He doesn't think it is fair that people who work have to pay a higher tax rate than people who make the same amount of money by investing. In fact, he said that he pays a lower tax rate than his secretary. What does he mean by that? Warren makes almost all of his money from capital gains – by selling investments that have gone up in value. His secretary makes all of her income by working a job. You know the IRS takes a greater percentage of money people make through ordinary income than they take of investments going up in value, such as capital gain income. It's crazy but true.

Want to know something else that's true?

I make a dish with lentils, peas, corn, and beans. It's really healthy but doesn't have a lot of taste to it. If I'm eating my last bowl of this dish and my daughter strolls by, guess what she'll do? She'll keep on a strollin'! She wants nothing to do with my lentil concoction.

Now, if only there were a type of income that the IRS didn't want a piece of. If only there were lentil income! And, hallelujah, there is! But you have to wait for the next lesson. Sorry!

WHAT'S SO SPECIAL ABOUT MUNICIPAL BONDS?

This is almost too good to be true

Quick recap. Ordinary income is income from most sources, like your job. It's taxed the most. Capital gains are what happens when you sell an investment for more than you bought it for. These are also taxed, but not as much as ordinary income.

And then there is this. It's a highly secretive investment. Some of the wealthiest families in the country know about this, but it requires opening an offshore bank account and funneling money through the Caymans into a wholly owned subsidiary that . . . just kidding!

No thanks!

Although some of the wealthiest families do invest in what I'm about to share with you, it is not really a secret and it doesn't require an offshore account or funneling of money anywhere. It's pretty straightforward and easy for anyone to do.

It's called municipal bond income! Let's break it down. Municipal. What does that mean? It means a city or state. What's a bond? An investment where you lend money.

So city/state + bond.

Municipal bonds aren't taxed!

You lend money to a city or state and all that wonderful interest income they pay you? That's pure lentils! The IRS plugs their collective noses and goes on a strollin' past you. They don't want any part of this income. It's all yours.

Pop quiz. How much tax will you pay if you make $100 in municipal bond income?

$0

Now rank these from who pays the most to who pays the least:

1) Capital gain from selling a mutual fund

2) Income you get from working a job

3) Municipal bond interest

The correct order is 2, 1, and 3.

Okay, the takeaways. My daughter likes pizza, and the IRS is not really fair or consistent in how they view income or how they tax it. Ordinary income is income from work, business, selling products, and interest you earn on your investments. Ordinary income is taxed the highest. Next are capital gains. These are gains from selling an investment for more than you bought it for. These are taxed, but not as much as ordinary income. Finally, we'll save the best for last. Bonds from cities or states are called municipal bonds. What makes these unique is that any interest you get from these are tax-free! These are the lentils of the income world. The IRS doesn't want any part of this income.

Maybe we had it all wrong about the IRS. Maybe they are good guys after all. Could it be? We shall see in the next lesson . . .

SO I'M TAXED IF I MAKE MONEY, BUT WHAT IF I LOSE MONEY?

There's good news and bad news…

As an investor, you are guaranteed to make money, right? That would be nice, but we know you can and will lose money on some investments. So what happens if you buy a stock at $100 and then sell it later for $75? After you have a good cry, you then need to figure out how much your loss is. Fortunately, this is 3rd grade math simple. You lost $25.

Couple of things to know here:

First, you bought the stock at $100. Instead of saying, "That's what I bought it for," we say your basis is $100. Basis is important because that's how you know if you've gained or lost money. When you first buy an investment, what you paid is typically your basis. But, over time, your basis can change.

For example, let's say you buy a rental house for $250,000. Your basis in the rental house is $250,000. But then you have to fix up the house and yard for $25,000. All the money you spent on those improvements is added to your original basis, so now your new basis is $275,000. Why is this important? Taxes, of course! If we didn't have

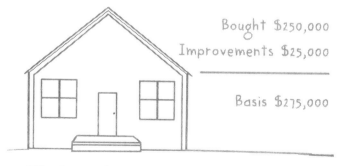

Bought $250,000
Improvements $25,000
_____
Basis $275,000

Why is your basis important? Taxes, of course!

to pay taxes on our gains, it wouldn't really matter. But let's say you sell the house for $300,000. All of a sudden, we care what the basis is. If it's $250,000, then we have a capital gain of $50,000. But if the basis is $275,000, then our gain is only $25,000. That's a big difference.

Today, firms such as Schwab or Fidelity where you invest in stock, bond, and mutual fund investments will keep track of your basis for you. In fact, if you go online to your investments, they will have a link where you can see all of your investments and the basis and gain/loss for each. It's pretty slick and it gives you a quick snapshot of what you have and what your gains or losses are for each investment, as well as for your whole account.

Okay, back to the investment you bought for $100 and sold for $75. Is it a gain or loss? Correct. You have a capital loss of $25. This is important because you may be able to do some cool tax tricks with this loss.

Each year, as you know, you have to file your taxes. This is the 1040 tax return where you have to list all your income and other items. Each year, you also have to tell the IRS if you had any gains or losses on your investments. But what if you have gains and losses on different investments? You made $100 on one investment but lost $25 on another. The IRS lets you net all your gains and losses together. So even though you had this $100 gain, you can subtract the $25 loss from this and end up with just a $75 capital gain that gets taxed. Of course, there are lots of rules and details, but that's the gist.

So what's the number one question everyone has on April 15? If you don't know already, you're going to next.

HOW DO I KNOW
HOW MUCH TO PAY IN TAXES?

They sure don't make it easy

I've thought about writing a book called *Everything You Need to Know about Income Tax*, but it turns out, someone already did. It's called the tax code, and it consists of rules, explanations, formulas, and opinions on all things related to the federal income tax. You won't believe how many pages it is.

73,954 – That's bigger than a *Harry Potter* book!

Yes, seriously. And get this. Remember how Einstein said the hardest thing in the world to understand is income tax? Well, when he died, the tax code was "only" about 15,000 pages. What would he say now?

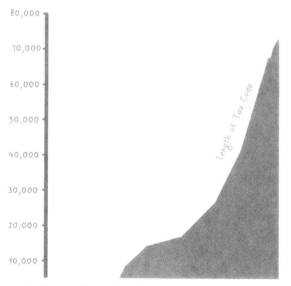

And you thought things were bad in the 50's

So what do we know so far about income taxes? (1) We have to pay the tax or we go to jail, and (2) it's very difficult to determine how much tax we have to pay. Nothing like setting us up for failure!

So how do we figure out how much we owe? Remember back in math class where the teacher would bark, "Show your work?" Think of the IRS as your cranky, old math teacher. We have to show our work on a form the IRS provides where we enter how much money we made and a few other things, and then we can figure out how much tax we owe. Not only that, but we have to do this every year.

The IRS tax form is called your income tax return. There are actually a couple of different kinds of these forms, but the most common is called the 1040. Why is it called the 1040 and not the 1041 or maybe something a little less nerdy like "The IRS Income Tax Form"? Laziness, really. When the government created the form way back in 1913, the government already used Form 1038, 1039, and the next available forms control number was, you guessed it, 1040.

Anyway, this 1040 is only two pages long, but it's a big deal. It's like when your girlfriend or wife says, "We need to talk." On the surface, it seems pretty harmless and simple, but underneath, there is a lot going on. It starts off pretty simple with name and contact information and then gets into more details.

What do you need to know about the 1040?

The takeaway for now is that the federal government, through the IRS, requires us to pay tax on the money we make. Figuring out how much we owe can be quite complex. The IRS makes us show our work using a two-page form called a 1040. On this form, we tell them how much we made and other things and then how much we owe. Oh, and we have to complete this form and send it in every single year.

HOW TO FILE YOUR TAXES

You've got three options…

There are really only three options when it comes to filing your taxes each year.

1. **Don't file your taxes.** Although this one is a real time saver in the short-run, prison can really ruin a perfectly good day. So that leaves just two options.

2. **Do it yourself.** For simple situations, you could probably sharpen a #2 pencil, fire up a calculator, and complete the form yourself. Or, you could use any one of the many software programs or websites to help you. Some of these are really easy to use and do a good job completing the tax return for you.

3. **Hire someone.** If doing your own tax return doesn't sound like a good use of a spring afternoon, you could hire someone to do it for you. There are several different types of people who could help. There are tax return preparers. Can you guess what they do? Bingo! They prepare tax returns. You give them your statements and they plug the numbers into their software, hit print, and you sign the 1040 and call it a day. Higher up the tax sophistication ladder are Enrolled Agents and CPAs. These guys and gals have a broader and deeper knowledge of taxes, and rather than just entering the numbers you give them, Enrolled Agents and CPAs, at least the good ones, can help you strategize and save taxes. How? They can recommend different options for you that might reduce your income, increase your deductions, or help you qualify for certain credits. You are hiring them for their expertise in reducing taxes, not just plugging in numbers.

So here's the distinction: if you want to file your taxes correctly, you can probably do it yourself with software or get someone to plug the numbers in for you. For very simple situations, that may be all that is necessary. But, for the vast majority of people and situations, it makes sense to spend the money to hire someone; not just to file your taxes correctly, but to file your taxes correctly while saving you as much tax as is legally possible.

That's the one you want. You may spend a few hundred dollars more, but if you can save a thousand or ten thousand dollars, it is well worth it.

The takeaway? Work with an Enrolled Agent or a CPA by default and only do it yourself if your situation is so simple that an Enrolled Agent or CPA tells you not to waste their time and that you could do it yourself.

WHY A 5% RETURN MAY BE BETTER THAN A 7% RETURN

This is the Twilight Zone chapter

How could a 5% return be better than a 7% return? You're about to enter a new dimension, a dimension of sound, a dimension of sight, a dimension of mind . . .

Want to impress your friends and advisors? Want to make more money? This lesson is for you.

The question is can a 5% return be better than a 7% return? The answer is a resounding yes!

How is that possible?

It's actually rather simple. I'll show you.

There's an old saying: it's not how much you make; it's how much you keep. It doesn't matter what your return is. Rather, what matters is your return after you pay any taxes. That's where the rubber meets the road. It's this after-tax return that is real. That's the money you can put in your pocket.

So don't be confused or misled by promises of high returns. Many mutual funds or advisors will say, "We got our clients a 10% return last year." Okay, but that is a bit meaningless. What they don't say is, "To get the 10% return last year, we generated a lot of taxes, so your after-tax return is probably more like 5%." Doesn't sound as impressive now, does it?

Look at after-tax returns. That's the true return you received.

HELP SMART

Section 6

GAME TIME!
WHO'S ON YOUR TEAM?

You'll want these three all-stars working for you

You can do it! This is the age of information and access. There has never been a better time to take control of your finances yourself than right now. You don't need help! You can do it all yourself!

That sure sounds good, doesn't it? But it's a bunch of hype and it's potentially damaging to your finances. Trust me; I've seen it many times.

But it's cool if you are one of those DIY lone wolf kinds of guys. If you want to do a lot of it yourself, you definitely can, but just be open to help. It's impossible to know and do everything. This stuff is too complex and there's too much money on the table to mess around. It's easy to get caught picking up pennies in front of a steamroller or whatever that saying is. I've been involved in finance, investments, and financial planning for nearly 20 years and I get help.

Advisor Triad

The question is what kind of help should you seek? There are a few different types of advisors that could be on your team – I call them THE ADVISOR TRIAD!

Legal. Why would you need an attorney? No, that's not a rhetorical question. You'll need an estate planning attorney to help you create your estate plan, which we'll talk about later. You may need a tax attorney for tax matters, or maybe a general business attorney if you start a company.

Who's on your team?

There are lots of different kinds of attorneys and there are many reasons you may need one from time to time.

Here's a bit of trivia for you. What's the difference between an attorney and a lawyer? A lawyer is someone who has graduated from law school. An attorney is someone who has graduated from law school and is licensed to practice law.

Tax. Because taxes will most likely be one of your biggest expenses, it makes sense to get an expert on your team who can help you not just file your taxes, but also help you legally reduce your taxes. For this, you may work with a CPA or an Enrolled Agent. This person will be, or at least should be, a key member of your team. With just one simple strategy or suggestion, they can cover their fees many times over.

Financial. Financial folks come in two flavors. There are the investment only guys. These are the people who don't really care much about your taxes, won't ask you many questions about your retirement goals, and will not spend any time on helping you make smart financial decisions. They are 100% focused on investments. If you have a question about asset allocation, they can answer it. If you have a question about the best retirement account to minimize taxes, you might as well ask Siri instead.

The second type of financial person is the comprehensive financial planner. This is the person who looks at your entire financial situation and can advise you on budgeting, estate planning, tax planning, retirement, and yes, most also can manage your investments as well.

If I had to choose, I'd always go with the comprehensive financial planner. Why? Because I am one and I'm biased. Besides that, I think to get the biggest bang from your finances and to make the best decisions, you need someone who sees how all the pieces fit together and who knows how what you do over here will affect what happens over there.

Pop quiz! If you are in a high tax bracket and want to lower your taxes, should you invest in municipal bonds? True or false? If you recall, the unique thing about interest income from municipal bonds is that it is, what? Tax-free! So, true. You'd want to invest in municipal bonds. If your investment only guy isn't aware of your tax situation, they may invest you in taxable bonds. It pays to have someone looking at and providing advice on everything.

Okay, so, what's the lesson here? The best and most successful professional athletes all have coaches, people they hire to help them perform better. When it comes to your finances, you might also benefit from hiring a coach or two. The three most common areas are tax, legal, and financial.

If you had to start with one, I'd suggest starting with a comprehensive financial planner, but with hundreds of thousands of people calling themselves financial planners, how can you find the right one for you? Is it possible that I keep asking these annoying rhetorical questions at the end of each lesson to keep you reading? Argh! Another rhetorical question. I can't help myself!

HOW TO FIND A GOOD FINANCIAL ADVISOR - PART 1

Here's how to eliminate 95% of advisors

So you want to find a good financial advisor? Okay, that's great. You want someone to work with you and help you make good financial decisions. Excellent!

There's just one problem. There are hundreds of thousands of financial advisors out there. How are you going to find the one who is right for you?

If you're an overachiever, you may have noticed there are three chapters on this topic. That seems like a lot. But here's the thing. Working with a good financial advisor can make the difference between success and failure. It makes sense that you find the right one to oversee your financial future.

I wish I could sit down with you and help you find the right advisor, but instead, I'm going to give you seven simple requirements in the next four lessons that will help you eliminate 95% or more of the advisors out there and leave you with the cream of the crop from which to choose.

There are seven criteria for finding a good financial advisor. Here's the first one:

Criteria 1 – Hire a Fiduciary

Oh, man. Really? That's how the list starts? Hire a fiduciary? What the heck is a fiduciary? Okay, how can I make this simple? There are two broad categories of advisors – fiduciaries and non-fiduciaries. Fiduciaries are legally obligated to put their clients' interests first, whereas non-fiduciaries can offer advice that is not in your interest as long as it is "suitable" to you. Clearly, it behooves you to work with an advisor who will always put your interests first, ahead of their own interests and of the firm they work for. Surprisingly (or maybe not so surprisingly), almost all of the big brokerage firms you see advertising on TV are not fiduciaries. They can put their (financial) interests ahead of the client, and this is perfectly acceptable, as long as they meet the minimum requirement of it being suitable to you. Don't settle for suitable. Hire a fiduciary.

Criteria 2 – Use Only Big Custodians

One of my favorite shows on TV is *American Greed.* This is a show where unsuspecting people got bilked out of their life savings by unscrupulous advisors. It's sad, very sad. One way to protect yourself is to make sure your investments are held at a big custodian. What does this mean? Basically, you want your money to be at a separate and unrelated firm from your investment advisor. For example, my clients don't send money to Pacifica Wealth Advisors; they send it to Schwab or Fidelity. I can still help them invest and manage their investments, but the money is not at my firm. The benefit from this is that this separate custodian will send you monthly statements. This way you can see exactly what is happening in your accounts.

Is that all you need to know? Not quite. You're going to learn about three little letters that separate the boys from the girls. Or the men from the girls. Or the men from the boys. Whatever. It's good and you're going to learn about it.

HOW TO FIND A GOOD FINANCIAL ADVISOR - PART 2

Three letters you want to look for

Pop quiz. Quick, which of the following is not a real financial designation?

- Life Underwriter Training Council Fellow

- Chartered Mutual Fund Counselor

- Certified Senior Consultant

- Certified Fund Specialist

They are actually all real! And trust me, I use the term "real" very generously.

So what does this mean? It means there are a whole lot of "professional designations" available to financial advisors to make them sound like they know what they are talking about, but there are really only a handful with any real meaning. And this brings me to . . .

Criteria 3 – Hire a Certified Financial Planner™ Practitioner

The hero you've been waiting for

This message brought to you by the Certified Financial Planner™ (CFP®) organization. No, not really! But this is a great way to narrow your search. A financial planner who has their CFP® designation has earned it by passing a comprehensive exam, completing a series of courses, agreeing to a code of ethics, and having three years' worth of professional experience in financial planning.

I'm sure I'll take heat from the Personal Retirement Planning Specialist group (yes, this is yet another designation), but the CFP® mark is arguably the most recognized comprehensive financial planning designation available. Are there other designations? Yes, literally hundreds. Some are good and some, as you've seen in the quiz, are bordering on the ridiculous.

At a minimum, your financial planner should have the CFP®. Are there bad financial advisors with the CFP®? Yes. Are there good financial advisors without the CFP®? Yes. But as a rule of thumb, get yourself a CFP®.

And here's a bit of a bonus for you. The CFP® represents the minimum. It's like thinking you're qualified to race in the Indy 500 because you have a driver's license. It's a good starting point, but with your financial life on the line, don't settle for the minimum.

Look for your advisor to have advanced designations or degrees, including a JD (law degree); CPA/EA (tax); CFA/CIMA (portfolio design and investment analysis); master's degree in tax, financial planning, economics, or finance; an MBA with an emphasis in finance/investments; or the PFS/CPWA (financial planning).

Okay, got it? At a minimum, make sure that if you are looking for a comprehensive financial advisor, he or she has a CFP® designation.

Excellent. Find an advisory with the CFP®. Done? Almost. In the next lesson, we'll go over four more key things you need to know to get the best advisor for you.

HOW TO FIND A GOOD FINANCIAL ADVISOR - PART 3

The remaining four things to look out for...

In your quest for a good financial advisor, we know we want to work with a fiduciary, a separate custodian, and someone who has their CFP® designation. Is that it? Not quite, but we're getting close.

Criteria 4 – Stick to the 10,000 Hour Rule

Psychologist Anders Ericsson has studied what makes great performers such great performers. His conclusion? Practice. Lots of practice, actually. The 10,000 hours of practice rule has emerged as a rule-of-thumb for how much practice is required to develop an expertise in a field of study. It often requires at least 10 years in one's profession to begin to have mastery. Again, this is a generality. If you were going in for open heart surgery, would you want a doctor to have 100 hours, 1,000 hours, or 10,000 hours? If I'm hiring a doctor or any specialist, I will only hire someone with at least 10 years of experience, and when you are hiring a financial advisor, attorney, or CPA, I strongly recommend you do the same.

Almost isn't good enough when it comes to your finances

Criteria 5 – Avoid Commission-Only Advisors

There are many different ways to pay for financial advice. You can pay by the hour, based on a percentage of assets the advisor manages for you (referred to as "AUM," or assets under management), a flat monthly retainer, commissions, or any combination of the above.

Commission-only advisors – usually stockbrokers and insurance salespeople today – should be avoided. Their entire financial livelihood is based on selling you something. You want your advisory team to be objective and to be your partner, not your adversary.

Stick with a fee-based advisor who charges an AUM fee and may receive incidental commissions on insurance products or a fee-only advisor who receives no commissions.

Criteria 6 – Check for a Clean Record

This one is so simple, but so few people do it. Most people do more research into choosing a restaurant than they will in choosing their financial advisor. But not you! You'll take the extra few minutes to check out any advisor you are thinking about trusting with your money, right?

Do a background check on your advisor to ensure there are no regulatory or legal infractions against him. Think of it as doing a Yelp check on your advisor. Go to https://brokercheck.finra.org for links you can use to check on the status of their license and regulatory history.

Also, don't rely on the bio your advisor provides you or the one on his website. If he claims to be a CFP® practitioner, verify it. If he claims he went to Yale, verify it. It takes just a moment, but it can save you dearly. Retired NFL star Ricky Williams learned this the hard way. He is suing his financial advisor for absconding with $6 million from his account and lying about being an attorney and a graduate of Harvard Business School. Don't blindly trust; verify instead.

Criteria 7 – Check Their Form ADV

Every Registered Investment Advisory firm must complete a document that discloses details about the firm, their clients, their experience, and other valuable information. This is a treasure trove of information as you evaluate advisors. Things to look for are an experienced team (at least 10 years of experience), good education and credentials, no negative legal issues, and a large pool of investor assets they manage. You can request a copy of the firm's Form ADV from the company itself or by going to adviserinfo.sec.gov.

But what happens after you find and start working with an advisor? How can you ensure that you make the most of that relationship? You're going to learn to think of the relationship in a whole new way.

WHEN TO BE THE FINANCIAL DRIVER OR PASSENGER

Start your engines . . .

Ying and yang. Chocolate and vanilla. Led Zeppelin and The Who. Throughout history, there have always been battles between two competing forces.

And now we can add driver versus passenger to that list. Here's what I mean.

Money can create an interesting power dynamic between you (the client) and your advisors. On one hand, it's your money and your life. Your advisors work for you, you are in charge, and you call the shots; you are the driver.

On the other hand, most people aren't comfortable enough with the tax code, laws, or financial strategies to make smart decisions. You must rely on your team to guide you; you are the passenger.

You shouldn't always rely on Uber

And this is what creates the driver versus passenger battle. Some people go too far one way or the other. For example, they may throw their hands up in the air and relinquish all control to their team because they feel confused and overwhelmed. Or on the flipside, they become involved in every detail and make it difficult for the experts to do their jobs. Both scenarios are disastrous. The key is to identify the areas where you will be the driver and the other areas where you will be the passenger.

So, what's someone to do? Here's what I've found that works best.

Be the driver when it comes to defining your goals, objectives, and vision. Sometimes, well-meaning attorneys, CPAs, and financial planners will place a higher emphasis on form over function. They may devise sophisticated strategies that are financially correct, but in doing so, compromise your overall vision and desire for simplicity. They may dazzle you with big words and highly technical details, but make sure you are vocal about what you want.

It also makes sense to be the driver when it comes to setting expectations for your team. It is worth repeating: your advisors work for you. It doesn't matter how little education or experience you have, or how many letters they have after their name, you pay them to perform a service. As a result, you should set expectations, such as how often to meet, how they should best communicate with you, and how well they should explain things.

Be the driver as it relates to asking questions and ensuring you understand what is happening. Every question you have is valid and deserves an explanation. What is "obvious" or "common sense" to them may not be to you. Don't be shy about asking a lot of questions or having your advisors explain things until you understand them.

You shouldn't attempt to be the driver in every situation, however. There is a reason you are hiring the best attorneys, CPA, and financial advisor you can find. They have decades (or should!) of knowledge and experience. You're paying them, so let them do their jobs. This means giving them the freedom to explore different strategies, to have conference calls with the other members of your team, and to keep an open-mind to their ideas and advice.

I've found that the best client relationships are the ones where the client paints the big picture of what they want and hope to achieve, and then lets the advisors craft the strategy for how to make that happen. Focus on the destination while you let your team figure out how to best get you there.

109

HOW I SEE THE WORLD . . .

It's hammer time!

And now, a short screenplay break.

FADE IN

EXT. WORKSHOP – DAY

NAIL

Hey there, Hank! How's it swingin'?

HAMMER

You know me. I'm swingin' just fine.

NAIL

Can you help me?

HAMMER

Of course, darling.

Hammer hits Nail into a large wooden board.

NAIL

Thanks, Hank!

HAMMER

Always happy to help.

INT. WORKSHOP – DAY

LIGHT BULB

Hey, sweetie.

HAMMER

Well, hello, pretty darling.

LIGHT BULB

Can you screw me into this light socket?

HAMMER

Of course. I'm happy to help.

Hammer smashes Light Bulb and then cries out.

HAMMER (yelling)

Noooo! Not again!

VOICEOVER

When you are a hammer, everything looks like a nail.

FADE OUT.

<u>THE END</u>

A tragic love story for the ages

Poor Hank. He killed his one true love. The voluptuous Barbie the Bulb. Why? Well, he had good intentions. He wanted to help, but all Hank was good for was one thing. When you see the world through the eyes of a hammer, the solution is always the same.

When it comes to your money, you have to watch out for the Hanks of the world.

Your job is to get into the mind of the advisor and to imagine how they see the world. Each financial specialist thinks of whatever they sell as the one grand solution to everything. If you're talking to a life insurance person, everything can be solved with life insurance. Need to pay for your kids' college? There's a life insurance policy for that. Need income during retirement? No problem. There's a life insurance policy for that. Need to save on taxes? There's a life insurance policy for that. Need to lose some weight? There's a life insurance policy for that.

Channel your inner Clarice. Get into the mind of the advisor. Figure out what they sell and how they are paid. If you know these two things, you can quickly see how they see the world.

The goal is to be aware of who is giving the advice, why they are giving it, and to make sure you are working with someone who sees the world clearly and can offer solutions that make sense, not just that make money for the advisor.

The takeaway? Don't let a Hank smash your finances.

Speaking of advisor Hank, wouldn't you like to know how he gets paid? I'm going to pull back the curtain and share with you exactly how financial advisors get paid next.

110

HOW ARE ADVISORS COMPENSATED?

Understand these four common fees...

The many ways an advisor can be compensated

Ah, very good question! Let's talk about the ways an investment advisor or financial planner can be compensated.

Hourly Fee. This is the easiest to understand. You get together and pay the advisor for their time. I guess the advantage of this is you control the cost. You know exactly what you are paying. The disadvantage is that even though you may need help, you may be reluctant to pick up the phone or ask for help, knowing that the clock is ticking. Also, what you think may only take an hour could easily swell into two, three, or more hours.

Flat Dollar Fee. Instead of charging by the hour, some advisors will charge a flat project fee – for example, if they are going to create a financial plan for you – or a flat monthly or quarterly fee. Flat fees can be good because you know what you're on the hook for going in, and you don't have to worry about tracking the minutes.

Commissions. What are commissions? It's basically a fee someone gets for buying or selling something for you, like if you need life insurance. An advisor can help you get a policy. For his efforts, he may get a commission, or a fee, when you buy it. Or maybe you want to sell 100 shares of McDonald's stock. Your advisor will sell these for you but may get a commission, or again, a fee, for doing so. When you think of a commission, think in terms of a transaction. Something happened. Something was bought or sold. Commissions can be a flat amount, or often, they are a percentage of whatever it is you are buying or selling. For example, if you sell your house, you may pay your real estate agent a commission. This could be 5% of the value of your house if they sell it for you. So if your house is sold for $100,000, then the real estate agent's commission would be $5,000. If your house was sold for $200,000, then 5% of this would be a commission or fee of $10,000.

Assets Under Management Fee. This is a common way advisors are compensated. If you really want to sound cool, you can say "AUM." This fee is not based on hours or transactions, but instead, it is a flat percentage of the assets your advisor is managing for you. Huh? Okay, let's break it down because it's actually much easier to understand than you think. Let's say you work with an investment advisor, and that advisor says she is going to charge you 1% AUM. What does that mean? It means that whatever assets she is managing for you, she gets a 1% per year fee. If you have an investment account with $100,000 in it, she would get a fee of $1,000 per year. Because an assets under management fee is so common, let's dig a bit deeper so you really understand it.

The first question you might have is, "What do you mean by 'assets under management'?" Does that include your house? Your Ford Fiesta? Your baseball card collection? The answer would be no. The assets we're talking about with this fee are investment assets. Not your house, personal items, or even your bank accounts. We're just talking about investments.

Okay, but what does it mean "under management"? Does your advisor supervise, have control over, or provide advice on the assets? For example, maybe you have two investment accounts, but your advisor only buys and sells investments in one of them. Well, that one would be the one "under management," meaning it is under her watchful eye and she is managing, or buying and selling, for you. The other investment account would not be under management and her fee would not apply to that account.

Those are the most common types of fee arrangements you will see. Keep in mind, though, that sometimes you get what you pay for and sometimes you don't. Meaning, just because you are paying high fees doesn't mean you are getting any better service or advice. In fact, if the fees you are paying are too high, it can make it difficult to make money as an investor.

Assume you will pay some fees. Find an advisor and a fee arrangement that you understand and that you are most comfortable with.

PROTECT SMART

Section 7

WHAT YOU NEED TO KNOW ABOUT PROPERTY AND CASUALTY INSURANCE

It takes the gecko 15 minutes, but it only takes me five

No one cares about this stuff, but it's also super important.

I'm going to make this short and sweet and give you just what you need to know and nothing more. You'll know more about insurance than 95% of the population in about five minutes.

First thing to understand: there are two main categories of insurance. Insurance for stuff and insurance for people.

In this lesson, you're going to learn about insurance for stuff, and the good news is that you already know something about this. Two common types of stuff insurance, more commonly called property and casualty or P&C insurance, are auto insurance and homeowner's insurance.

You may already have this kind of insurance, but why? Why have stuff insurance? Everyone says you need it, so you get it? Doesn't insurance seem like a waste? You're paying your hard earned money for what? The truth is that insurance is a waste . . . until it's not a waste.

Here's what I mean. You get a bill a couple of times a year and reluctantly pay it. But what do you get? Probably nothing, zilch, nada, zip, zero. So, on one hand, you are paying for something and not getting anything in return.

But the best insurance is the kind of insurance you pay for and never need. Because when you actually use insurance, something bad has happened. Think about it. If you use your auto insurance, you've probably been involved in an accident. If you use your homeowner's insurance, your house probably burnt to the ground or a tree has fallen on it.

The only thing worse than paying for insurance and never needing it is paying for insurance and needing it.

But what are you really getting with stuff insurance – that is, property and casualty insurance? You pay a little bit, called a premium, to protect an expensive asset.

Pop Quiz: Which of the following would it make sense to have insurance for?

- Lawn chair

- Diamond ring

- House

- Car

- Miley Cyrus CD collection

It only makes sense to have insurance on expensive assets, where it would be really expensive for you to replace it if something happened. So the answers are obviously your diamond ring, house, and car. I don't care how big your Miley Cyrus CD collection is; it's definitely not worth having insurance for it.

But so far, we've only talked about getting insurance on stuff, on things like jewelry, cars, and houses. There is another type of P&C insurance which could not be more important that you absolutely, positively, definitely will want to know about and have because if you don't, your entire financial future could go up in flames. How's that for a teaser for the next lesson?

112

UMBRELLA LIABILITY INSURANCE

The least understood but most important type of insurance

When it rains, it pours. That's why an umbrella liability insurance policy is worth its weight in gold.

I grew up in the Pacific Northwest where it rains. Not a little, but a lot. That's why I'm such a big fan of something called umbrella liability insurance. If you're like me, you go through a lot of umbrellas. You lose them, or in a heavy wind they do that flipping thing and then get ruined. Well, fret no longer. You can get umbrella insurance! Just like auto insurance covers your car and homeowner's covers your house, umbrella insurance covers your umbrella.

What? All right, I'm just kidding. Basically, take everything I said about umbrella insurance and forget it.

Umbrella liability insurance does not actually insure your umbrella. It does something much cooler and, some would argue, a lot more important. And if you consider not ruining your finances and being dead broke for the rest of your life more important than having a good working umbrella, then sure, I guess it's more important.

Here's how umbrella liability insurance works. The key word is liability. What is liability? It's basically when something goes bad and you're responsible for making it better again. Here's an example: you crash your car into another car. Okay, so your auto insurance will pay to fix up your car and the car you hit. That makes sense. But what if the person you hit got really hurt? They might sue you. You hit them with your car, so your auto insurance should cover this. And guess what? It does. Yeah! But, not so fast.

Quiz. What's the minimum liability you need on an auto policy in California?

$500,000

$350,000

$250,000

$15,000 ▪ this is the correct answer

Well, what happens if you get sued for $1 million and your policy goes up to $250,000? No problem. You tell the person suing you that your insurance will only pay $250,000, and then they reduce the lawsuit against you down to $250,000. That's sweet of them. And that's total fantasyland. Ain't gonna happen. Here's what would happen. Your auto insurance company pays them $250,000, and then you become responsible for paying them the remaining $750,000. Yup. You might have to sell your stocks and bonds, maybe your house, and if that's not enough, they might take part of your paycheck each month until you've paid off the whole amount. That, my friends, is a nightmare. You work decades earning, saving, and making smart decisions, and then, because you decide you need a gallon of milk from the store, you lose it all in the blink of an eye.

Enter umbrella insurance, sometimes called personal liability insurance. It's super cheap, about $250 a year for $1 million worth of coverage.

I normally don't like telling people what to do – okay, who am I kidding? I love telling people what to do, but I usually am better at resisting the temptation. I can't resist here, though, because the lesson is too important. You absolutely must have an umbrella liability policy. Must, must, must. This is one of those no brainers.

Call the insurance company where you have your auto or homeowner's insurance and tell them you want to add this. Okay, but how much? The minimum is $1 million. I know that sounds like a lot, but it's only $250 a year and if someone sues you, there is a good chance it will be for a lot. If you have significant assets, get more. I have clients with $20 million umbrella liability policies.

Why are you still reading this? Stop it! Pick up the phone and get this cheap protection now!

113

ALL ABOUT LIFE INSURANCE

It's really pretty simple...

Earlier I said there were two categories of insurance. One is for stuff and the other is for people. We did the stuff thing; now it's all about you!

There are lots of different kinds of insurance for people.

Insurance for people, as you could guess, is insurance on a person. Let's go through the main types: Health, life, and disability.

Health – Not much to explain here. You already understand this one. You pay premiums, and if you get sick or hurt, the insurance company helps pay the medical bills.

Life – Now, with this one, there is more to explain. It's not quite as understood. Basically, if you die, then the insurance company pays whoever you want some money. Sounds kind of sick, doesn't it? But there are some really important uses for life insurance.

Let's pull back the onion layers a bit here and get down to the basics.

The cost of the insurance, the amount you pay, is called the **premium.**

The **benefit**, also called the death benefit, is the money the insurance company pays when you die.

The **insured** is the person who is insured. If they die, then the insurance company has to pay.

The **beneficiary** is the person who gets the money; it is the person the insurance company pays if the insured dies.

There are probably hundreds of types of life insurance, but the good news is you really need to only know the two big categories. There is term life insurance and then there is permanent life insurance. That's it! Just those two.

So what is term life insurance? It's basically a policy that you buy for a certain number of years, and at the end of the term, you no longer have the life insurance. Some people call it renting a life insurance policy. Imagine renting an apartment. You don't really own it, but if you pay your rent each month, your lease is good for one year. At the end of the year, the landlord can kick you out. The most common lengths of term insurance are 10 years, 20 years, and 30 years. What this means is that if I have a 20 year term insurance policy, as long as I pay the fee, the premium, to the insurance company each year, I am guaranteed to have this policy for the next 20 years. If I die over the next 20 years, then the insurance company has to pay my beneficiary. But what if I die 20 years and one day later? Who does the insurance company pay? Sadly, no one because your 20 year term policy expired. It vanished. It went away at the end of the 20 years. It's like a carton of milk with an expiration date. Once that date comes, the milk is bad and you can't use it anymore.

So why would anyone want a disappearing life insurance policy? It's cheap. You can get quite a big death benefit for very little premium. And this can make sense for a lot of people. Let's say it's a young family and they don't have a lot of money to spend on insurance. They can get a cheap term life insurance policy and if the dad dies, then the insurance company can pay the mom.

Okay, so that's term insurance. Cheap and it has an expiration date.

So if you had to guess what permanent life insurance is, what might you say? The keyword here is permanent. Unlike term insurance that has a limited term, permanent insurance is forever. As long as you pay the premiums, this insurance has no expiration date.

Pop Quiz: If you had a permanent insurance policy, which of the following will the insurance company pay if you die?

- 10 years

- 20 years + 1 day

- 32 years

- 87 years + 6 days

All of the above!

It sounds like permanent life insurance is the way to go because it never goes away, but, of course, what do you think the downside is?

It's more expensive. Quite a bit more expensive, actually. But, it can definitely make sense in the right circumstances.

Okay. Got it? Life insurance comes in two flavors. One that melts and goes away (term), and the other that stays forever (permanent). Term is less expensive, and permanent is more expensive.

Is there job insurance? Stay tuned.

114

ALL ABOUT DISABILITY INSURANCE

This insurance can be a real life saver…

You are practically an expert at this insurance stuff by now. No, seriously. You probably know more than 90% of the population about insurance. Congrats! But there's one more type you should know about. It's called job insurance. Actually, that's not what it's called, but that's really what it does. The real name is disability insurance. Here's how it works.

You have a family and you are concerned that if something happened to you, your family would not have enough money to get by. So, you buy some cheap term insurance just in case something bad happens. You sleep soundly at night knowing you are protected.

Don't worry! As long as you have disability insurance, you'll be fine.

And then something bad happens. Maybe you fall off a ladder, get in an accident, get diagnosed with something, and you can't work anymore. The income from your job stops, but the bills keep coming in. The really bad news is you didn't die. Yeah, the problem is you're still alive. How is that a problem? That life insurance policy you have doesn't pay your family unless you die. So now you have no job, no income, can't work, and lots of bills.

Oh, man. Now what? The solution is disability insurance! Disability insurance will pay you if you get hurt or sick and can't work.

Disability insurance is very important. Why? Your chances of dying before you get old are really pretty small, but your chances of becoming disabled are much higher.

There are lots of different options and lengths with these policies, but you get the gist of it.

So, the takeaway is to be careful climbing on ladders and that disability insurance will pay you if you get sick or hurt and can't work.

TOP 3 RISKS TO YOUR MONEY

40 years to earn it; a moment to lose it

Once, I was preparing for a long bike ride – it was going to be nearly 60 miles. I put on my fancy bike shoes and spandex shorts, packed some energy bars, and secured a big water jug to the back of my bike. And off I went. A good hour into the ride, the sun was burning down and I was losing steam. I reached back and grabbed my water jug – desperate for some hydration to get me going again. And then I almost cried. My water jug was almost entirely empty. I forgot to put the cap on it, and the bumps and turns caused the water to spill out. Was I trekking across the Sahara Desert without water? Well, no. I just ran into a 7-Eleven and got more water. But still, I was getting pretty thirsty.

The takeaway is don't be dumb. Don't let a silly oversight ruin your plans. And when it comes to your money, what can take years and decades to save and invest can literally be stripped from you in an instant.

But don't be misled. The person who takes your money overnight won't sneak in through the backdoor wearing a ski mask and rob you. Oh, no. The person who takes your money will almost certainly be wearing a suit.

There are three main threats to your money:

1.   Divorce

2.   Lawsuit

3.   Fraud

Each of these can decimate your finances overnight. Can you prevent them? Well, no, actually. You can't prevent them from happening. You can't stop a divorce. You can't stop someone from suing you. And you can't keep someone from trying to defraud you. So even though you

The triple threat to your finances

are helpless from stopping any of these from happening, you have some very powerful things you can do to minimize the damage.

You can't prevent a car accident, but if you drive a five-star rated car, wear a seatbelt, and have plenty of airbags, you can certainly walk away from most accidents.

And that's really our goal here. Bad stuff happens to good people all the time. You can't change that. But if bad stuff happens to you, I want to know you've taken the steps to protect yourself and your finances.

Because let me tell you, the alternative is ugly. I've seen good people lose it all overnight. Please, please, please, let's make sure that doesn't happen to you.

Follow along in the next few chapters and you'll be fine.

HOW TO (FINANCIALLY) SURVIVE A DIVORCE

How to separate from your spouse, not your money

The only thing more heated and emotional than talking about divorce is talking about how to protect your assets in a divorce. Let me come clean so you know where I'm coming from, or maybe more accurately, not coming from.

I'm not going to show you how to take advantage of an unsuspecting spouse or get out of child support. My goal is to share with you a few strategies that have been used for decades to protect the assets that come into a marriage.

And many people assume these strategies are only used by rich guys and their new young wives. Not so. More and more women are implementing the ideas I'm going to share with you to protect themselves. A good friend of mine went through a divorce and is now on the hook for her ex-husband's credit card debt and student loans. Think about that. She now is on the hook for over $100k of debt that her ex-husband hid from her and she had no part of. If you have money and want to protect it if you get married and then divorced, this lesson is for you. Period.

Okay, now that I've given you that disclaimer, let's get into it.

Divorce and family law is incredibly complex and each state has their own quirky rules, but here's the good news. We can be near-experts at protecting your money from divorce by only knowing three things:

1. **Co-habitation Agreement.** A client once joked, "The best way to protect yourself from divorce is to never get married!" That's funny, no? Unfortunately, it's bad advice. His advice may protect you from many of the negative financial issues surrounding divorce, but even this extreme position won't protect you from all of the problems. Why? Many states have cohabitation laws or recognize common law marriage. This means that if you just live with your partner and never get married, you may have some financial liability if you separate and they move out.

   One way to protect yourself is to enter into a cohabitation agreement with your partner. A cohabitation agreement is a document that outlines how property, assets, and debt will be divided, as well as how financial support will be handled if you separate.

   So, if you are going to move in with someone, or if you are already living with someone, and you want to protect your money if you separate, speak to a family law attorney about the financial risks you face if the relationship dissolves. Find out if a cohabitation agreement makes sense for you.

2. **Prenuptial Agreement.** Okay, still not married yet. A prenuptial agreement (often called a "pre-nup" or a pre-marital agreement) is an agreement you enter into before marriage that spells out who owns what, how income earned during the marriage will be treated, whether there will be spousal support, and other issues. Without a pre-nup, your ex-spouse can be entitled to a large portion of your money. The laws are tricky and different in each state, but if you have a properly drafted pre-nup, it can save you hundreds of thousands or millions of dollars in legal fees, spousal support, and assets.

   Again, if you are interested in protecting your money from divorce, talk to a family law attorney.

3. **Gifts/Inheritance.** Okay, so whether you are married or not, or have a pre-nup or not, money that is gifted to you or money you receive from an inheritance may be protected in

a divorce. Part of it depends on the state you live in, but many states consider the gift or inheritance to be separate property as opposed to marital property. This just means that it's not part of the marital assets that get split up in a divorce, but instead, it's your separate property. That's the good news. But, you must keep the money or assets you get separate. That means you should open up a separate account in just your name. Don't mix them up in your joint account. There are some other rules and things to know, but for this lesson, just try to remember that if you are going to get a gift or inheritance, you should talk to a family law attorney to see what you should do to protect those assets in a divorce.

Okay, that was a bit of a long lesson and a little technical, but now you are aware of the three things that can protect you in a divorce or separation: a co-habitation agreement, a prenuptial agreement, and how gifts and inheritance may be special if you keep them separate.

All right, enough with the depressing divorce lesson. Let's move on to something much lighter and uplifting . . . getting sued! Yay!

HOW TO (FINANCIALLY) SURVIVE A LAWSUIT

The sound you never want to hear

Here's a sound you never want to hear: Imagine you are sitting at home one quiet evening and you get a knock at your door. You open the door and there is a stranger staring back at you who asks, "Are you so-and-so?" After answering yes, they respond, "You have just been served." You tremble as you take the package and then open it. It's a letter from blah, blah, blah attorney at law and the first sentence grabs you: "So-and-so is suing you for an undetermined amount." The rest of the words fade away.

An undetermined amount? Flashes of living under a bridge and eating out of a can flood your mind. How could this be happening to you?

Don't let a lawsuit ruin your life. Make sure you have an umbrella liability insurance policy as a first line of defense.

Lawsuits are absolutely terrifying, but if you haven't protected yourself, not only can they be terrifying, but they can also ruin your life. Your house? Gone. Your investments? Gone. Your bank account? Gone.

You can get sued by anyone, for anything, at any time. It's sick, I know, but it's true. Anyone can sue you for anything. This means what you've worked so hard to build can be wiped away with just one lawsuit.

Okay, so good luck with that. Oh, you want to know how to protect yourself? Of course you do! And the good news is that we've already talked about the solution. The very first layer of defense is to have an umbrella liability insurance policy. Remember that one, right? It's the inexpensive insurance that sits on top of your auto and homeowner's or renter's insurance. If you get sued, this little policy can go a very long way to protecting your assets. And for most people, this is all they need.

Are there more sophisticated asset protection strategies? In a word, abso-freakin-lutely. Lots of them. More than you would ever care to know, actually.

But for our purposes, just make sure you have that umbrella liability policy. Go get it!

118

HOW TO (FINANCIALLY) SURVIVE A FRAUDSTER

6 tips to protect yourself from the next Bernie Madoff

Bernie made off with lots of money. How can you protect yourself from fraud?

There is a date that will live in infamy. On December 11, 2008, anyone with an investment or bank account took a collective gasp. It was on this day that Bernie Madoff was arrested by the FBI on suspicion of committing the largest Ponzi scheme in history. Ultimately, thousands of clients were bilked out of billions of dollars. But, unfortunately, Bernie Madoff was not the only advisor stealing from clients. In the days and months that followed Madoff's arrest, hundreds of other Ponzi schemes were exposed.

As a long-time viewer of CNBC's television show *American Greed*, I see just how depraved some people can be.

There are numerous ways to lose your money, everything from divorce to spending too much or making bad investments, but fraud is a different animal. It's theft, plain and simple.

So how can you protect yourself? Here are a few things to always keep in mind if you are working with an investment advisor, attorney, or business manager.

1. **Don't be greedy.** This is the key takeaway. If something sounds too good to be true, I can assure you it is. If someone promises 15% returns no matter what, don't walk, run away. If you think to yourself, "Wow! I have to get in on this," then don't.

2. **Research your advisor.** The first place to start is by finding the right advisor. Do a background check and verify if they've ever had any regulatory issues. Your approach to getting an advisor should be to hire slow and fire fast. Take your time in finding the right person at the right company. If you sense any issues or wrongdoing, fire fast to avoid damage.

3. **Require phone confirmations on wires.** No money should be wired from your account to an account not in your name without a signature and verbal approval from you. This will help prevent unauthorized wires.

4. **Never sign blank forms.** Under no circumstances should you sign blank forms or documents.

5. **Separate custodian.** Your money should be held at a separate and unrelated firm from your investment advisor. Because Bernie Madoff was the investment advisor and held the assets, he was able to withdraw client funds and create fictitious monthly statements. Keep your assets at an unaffiliated company who will send you statements so you can see exactly what is happening in your accounts.

6. **Watch those statements.** Resist the temptation to toss the monthly investment statements into the drawer. Take the time to review the withdrawals and the account activity for suspicious activity.

Don't let this lesson scare you. The con men and rip-off artists represent just a tiny fraction of the advisors out there, but still, follow these six simple rules and you'll go a long way toward protecting your money.

Man. We've had three kinds of depressing chapters in a row – divorce, getting sued, and now fraudsters. Enough already. Let's move on to something much more pleasant to talk about, like death.

119

HOW TO (FINANCIALLY) SURVIVE DEATH

Your family will thank you…

What happens when you die? According to the Catholic tradition . . . no, don't worry. This is not a religious or philosophical discussion about what happens to you when you die. We want to know what happens to your stuff and your money when you die. Now that's interesting.

Think about it. A person was alive yesterday and that person had a kid, an Xbox, some IRA investments, a house, and a bank account. Today, that person is dead. But what happens to all that stuff?

Ask five friends and I bet you'll get five different answers.

You really have about three main options when it comes to handling what happens to your stuff after you die:

1. **Do nothing.**

2. **Will.**

3. **Trust.**

Do nothing. Well, this is surely the easiest . . . for you. But, for your family, this is definitely not the easiest. Why? Here's how it works. Either you write down where you want your stuff to go or the state you live in will decide. Yup. Each state has their own rules for what happens to someone's stuff when they die. It might go to your spouse, it might go to your kids, and it might go to your spouse and kids. It's all over the map. So this is a problem. What if you want your money to go somewhere else? Remember, either you say where you want your stuff to go or your state will. So doing nothing is not the best estate plan.

Will. Now this is getting better. A will is really just a letter where you say where you want your stuff to go and who gets what. You might say your brother gets $50,000 and your aunt gets your house. Whatever you want. That's the beauty with a will – you get to decide exactly who gets what. And you want to know something else? If you have kids, it is in your will where you decide who you want to look after them. That's huge. No, really. That is huge. If you die with young kids and did no estate planning, it's up to the courts to decide who takes care of your kids. This is a terrible outcome. The only solution is to name a guardian in your will.

Trust. Now we are getting a bit more sophisticated. A trust, often a called a living trust or family trust, is kind of like a will in that you get to say who gets what when you die. So if they are similar, why even bother with a trust? There are many reasons, but this is the most important.

You get to have a whole lot more say and control over your stuff after you die. With a will, it's basically, "So-and-so gets my $1 million investment account." End of story. But with a trust, you can say, "So-and-so gets my $1 million investment account, but they can only get $25,000 of it a year until they are 25 years old, and then they can get $50,000 a year until they are 30, but if they get a master's degree, then they can get $75,000 a year, etc." You have total control over who gets your stuff, how much they get, when they get it, and you can set certain restrictions. A lot of families will use a trust because with just a will, the kid would get the full $1 million when they turn 18. And parents think, maybe, just maybe, they may not make the best decisions with a $1 million at age 18. So, they'll set up a trust so Junior can't blow through all the money at 18.

Okay, so that's it? As my daughter likes to say, easy peezy lemon squeezy. Do nothing and let the state decide. Write a will. Or create a trust. At a minimum, you need a will, but if necessary, you can also have a trust. Capisce?

WHAT'S A BENEFICIARY?

A slick way to leave money to your family and friends...

I kind of lied to you. I know our relationship is built on trust, but when I told you your options for leaving your assets to others after you passed away were just to do nothing, write a will, or create a trust, I didn't tell you the whole truth. As my cheating girlfriend used to say, "It's not a lie. It's just an act of omission."

So, what is the mysterious fourth option you have when you want to leave your stuff to others after you die?

This option is mind numbingly easy. For your bank accounts and investment accounts, when you open the account, you can tell them where you want the account to go when you die. It can be an awkward conversation. "Welcome to our bank and thank you for opening an account with us. We hope we can serve you for many years to come, but if you croak tomorrow, what should we do with your money?"

Here's how it works. Let's say you have an IRA. You can name whoever you want to get the IRA if you die. You can even name two or three or however many people you want. You can say, "I want 60% to go to my mother, 20% to go to my brother, and 20% to go to the Humane Society." Bam! Done.

These people you list are called beneficiaries. When you open a new account, you might be asked, "Who do you want as primary and contingent beneficiaries?" Let's unpack this so it makes sense.

The **primary beneficiaries** are the people you want the account to go to first – that's why they are called primary.

But what if you list your best friend as your primary beneficiary, and you both die in a freak and tragic Russian roulette game? Get it? Freak and tragic like it was unexpected to die while playing

Russian roulette? You see, it's not freak and tragic. It's entirely expected.

Both you and your friend have died together. Now who gets your account? That's where the contingent beneficiary comes in. So you'd have your friend listed as primary and maybe your sister as contingent. You really want your best friend to get it if you die, but if he's dead, too, then your sister can have it.

Does this make sense?

There's one limitation to naming beneficiaries, though. Sadly, this won't work with your '67 Mustang or your house. It only works with bank accounts and investment accounts.

And here's some good news. Most people will have a will, maybe a trust as well, and will also name beneficiaries on their accounts. It's not about doing just one of these – you can and should use them all together.

CONCLUSION

You've built a financial foundation; here's what's next...

After working with some of the wealthiest people in the world, I've realized they think about money differently and do things with their money differently than others.

The first thing they all have in common is they have financial confidence. This doesn't mean they are experts in investing or tax and that they have all the answers, but they have a level of knowledge about finance that provides them with comfort and confidence.

Warren Buffett often says, "The more you learn, the more you earn." His advice for those who want to become wealthy? Learn the language of finance. He compares it to a foreign language: "Getting comfortable in a foreign language takes a little experience, a little study early on, but it pays off big later on."

Guess what? By reading *Get Money Smart*, you've done this! You've immersed yourself in the language of money and in the process you've become more financially confident. You no longer feel as nervous or scared when you think about investing or personal finance. You've built a solid foundation of financial knowledge that will last a lifetime.

The only thing left for you to do is to sign-up for the free video course at http://moneysmartcourse.com now. You will get access to new and exclusive content and maybe a surprise or two! Thank you for joining me on this journey. I hope to see you soon....

MONEY SMART VIDEO SERIES

BRING THE LESSONS TO LIFE!

FREE INSTANT ACCESS
WWW.MONEYSMARTCOURSE.COM

ABOUT THE AUTHOR

Get Money Smart

Hello, my name is Robert Pagliarini. I am the president of an investment and wealth management firm called Pacifica Wealth Advisors. We serve clients across the country and around the globe. We have developed a reputation for our specialized work with individuals, business owners, and sudden wealth recipients.

ALWAYS LEARNING

I've made it my mission to become a life-long learner and student, sometimes to the dismay of my family. I have several photos of me on my honeymoon lounging poolside, reading a thick book on wealth management. When on a non-profit trip to Myanmar, I studied on the plane for the IRS Enrolled Agent exam. When on vacation in Europe with my wife, I was caught highlighting a journal column on the taxation of lawsuit damages. I have a large purple folder marked "To Read" filled with columns and papers on investing, taxes, asset protection, and estate planning that I bring with me nearly everywhere. I love to learn, and I think it is a necessity if you want to provide the best advice and current strategies to clients. This probably explains all of the letters after my name. I am a Certified Financial Planner™ practitioner, a Certified Divorce Financial Analyst, an Enrolled Agent with the IRS, and have a Master's Degree in Financial Services. I'm currently working on earning my Ph.D. in financial and retirement planning.

PSYCHOLOGY OF MONEY

Although I've spent a great deal of time learning the financial, tax, and legal aspects of investing, financial planning, and sudden wealth, I would be doing my clients a huge disservice if I stopped there. Although I'm a financial advisor, I learned quickly that if I was going to really help my clients, I needed to understand the psychology of money, motivation, emotions, and relationships. To that end, I went back to school and earned a Master's Degree in Psychology with an emphasis in marriage and family therapy. This program required I conduct hundreds of hours of face-to-face counseling. To better connect with clients, I've graduated from business and personal coaching programs as well as workshops in Solution Focused Therapy and others. My goal is not to be a therapist for my clients; it is to better understand what drives them and to help them make the best financial decisions they can.

LOVE OF TEACHING

This is the fourth book I've written (fifth, if you count a free eBook I wrote during the 2008-2009 financial crisis). My first was the #1 bestselling *The Six-Day Financial Makeover: Transform Your Financial Life in Less Than a Week* (St. Martin's Press, 2006). I wrote this as a general guide for anyone who wasn't quite sure what they should be doing with their finances. Although the book is almost a decade old, the advice is still as relevant today as it was when I wrote it. My second book was *The Other 8 Hours: Maximize Your Free Time to Create New Wealth & Purpose* (St. Martin's Press, 2010). This book was a departure from traditional personal financial advice and was more focused on investing your human capital rather than investment capital. The third was *The Sudden Wealth Solution: 12 Principles to Transform Sudden Wealth into Lasting Wealth* (Harbinger Press, 2015). This book provides concrete solutions on how to manage the financial, tax, and psychological issues around sudden wealth.

I think books are a great medium for providing timeless advice, but rules and laws can change quickly. If you want to read my latest thoughts, I write financial columns for Forbes, Business Insider, AOL, The Huffington Post, and others.

DADDY ON TV

Over the years, I've had the privilege of appearing on Dr. Phil, 20/20, Good Morning America, Fox Business, Katie Couric, and many others. I always have a good time on these shows, and my daughter gets a kick out of seeing Daddy on TV.

HELPING THE LESS FORTUNATE

I'm not sure if it was because of my own experience as a child seeing my family struggle financially, but I've always been interested in helping those with less. I got in the habit of writing checks and supporting causes, but there was something missing – I wanted to do more. A few years ago, a couple of friends and I started a non-profit organization called The Band of Brothers Foundation. Our charity supports poor and often parentless children around the world. We currently have an active school, orphanage, and other projects in Thailand, Vietnam, Myanmar, Cambodia, Indonesia, and the Philippines. Visiting these countries and helping these kids has been one of the best things I've ever done.

MANY ADVENTURES

Traveling around South East Asia over the past several years ignited the adventurer in me. A couple of times a year, I travel to exotic places around the world. I've climbed Mt. Kilimanjaro, hiked the Inca Trail to Machu Picchu, hang-glided in Brazil, ice-climbed in Colorado, camped at the bottom of the Grand Canyon, mountain biked in Burma, trekked to the Great Wall of China, and explored the jungles of Thailand and Malaysia with friends and clients. Not all clients are interested in these trips, but they are always welcome.

I WANT TO HEAR FROM YOU

I've found that it is one thing to read a book and something quite different to implement the strategies recommended. If, after reading this book, you have a good handle on what you need to do, my mission will be accomplished. If you have additional questions or need help making the ideas in this book work for you, please do not hesitate to contact me. People are often surprised when I personally respond to an email or phone call. I do what I do because I love it. I'm happy to answer a question or point you in the right direction. At the very least, go to http://moneysmartcourse.com and signup for the free video course.

With warm regards,

Robert Pagliarini

Business Website: http://pacificawealth.com

Book Website: http://moneysmartcourse.com

Email: robert@pacificawealth.com

CPSIA information can be obtained
at www.ICGtesting.com
Printed in the USA
FSOW02n2217260118
43845FS